Guidelines for Online Success

"Success is not the key to happiness.
Happiness is the key to success.
If you love what you are doing,
you will be successful."

Albert Schweitzer (1875–1965)

Guidelines for Online Success

Ed. Rob Ford / Julius Wiedemann

TASCHEN

Guidelines for Online Success
Contents

Guidelines for Online Success

Introduction

by Rob Ford,
Favourite Website Awards (FWA)

00

Introduct

Have you ever wondered why your websites didn't quite match up to the success of your competitors or peers? Have you ever looked at other sites and thought: "Why didn't I think of that?" Well, let me open up a few new doors for you and some exciting new avenues for your online endeavours.

Firstly, let me give you a brief background on myself and the project I founded, Favourite Website Awards, and then I'll hand you over to many experts from around the world who will give you their unique perspective, insights and tips and tricks on how to achieve success online.

In 1997 I first started creating websites. Those were the days of animated GIFs and lake applets. Three years later I started to use Flash and began designing websites for small businesses who wanted to get on the whole interweb bandwagon. In the same year, 2000, my small agency website, treecity, was chosen as a finalist for the UK's top web award, the Yell UK Web Awards, and the buzz surrounding the whole event was incredible.

"In 1997 I first started creating websites. Those were the days of animated GIFs and lake applets."

In May 2000, I set up my own website awards project, Favourite Website Awards, with a sole focus on cutting edge web design and more specifically, sites using Flash. Favourite Website Awards quickly became recognised as FWA and eight years later it has grown into the most visited web award in history. With over 30 million site visits to date, FWA receives over one million site visits per month (and still rising). It has become widely recognised by the industry as the number one achievement for innovative web design through its Site Of The Year award. It was also named the number one web award in the world after winning the Best Web Awards Award from *The Chicago Tribune* in 2007, beating the likes of the Webby Awards and YouTube Video Awards.

The purpose of this book is to give you access to some of the best brains and most creative and forward thinking minds in the interactive world. There are contributors in this book who have won many of the world's top accolades for new media work, including Cannes Lions, Clio Awards, D&AD, FWA Site Of The Year, The One Show, Webby Awards, and more.

"This book is about how to succeed online and how you can gain an edge on your competitors and also win industry acclaim as well as respect from your peers."

Guidelines for Online Success will act as your bible on how to go the extra mile when creating websites and marketing your ideas and projects. It will provide you with technology, programming and technical advice as well as giving you an insight into the best ways to manage content and the whole e-commerce side of things.

You will gain unique perspectives from many different agencies across numerous countries, all of whom add to the wonderful mix of culture and creativity that makes the web such a colourful and inspiring place. For example, have you ever wondered why the Japanese have always been good at minimal expression? Maybe you have seen a weird and wacky website overflowing with character and personality that you will never forget? How about a website that boasts great logic and intelligent content management? Or even a website that just had incredibly clear sound playing on it? You can find out about all of these areas and many more, directly from the people who excel on these particular subjects.

Guidelines for Online Success is broken down into six chapters: Interface & Design; Marketing & Communication; Technology & Programming; Technical Advice; Content/Content Management; and E-Commerce.

Each chapter is introduced by someone we could all dream of having as a mentor and each chapter is broken down into a number of categories, all of which are individually introduced by different people, who are experts in their field from around the globe. Each category has some example websites, all hand picked by myself from my initial list of over two thousand award winning websites. They are what I would class as the best, most outstanding and influential examples of their kind.

Please remember that this book has been created to give you an extra edge when designing and developing and it is not an idiot's guide on how to build a website. This book is about how to succeed online and how you can gain an edge on your competitors and also win industry acclaim as well as respect from your peers.

"This is a universal book for people all over the world, just as the Internet is itself."

Guidelines for Online Success has website examples from over thirty countries with contributions from people in more than twenty countries. This is a universal book for people all over the world, just as the Internet is itself.

Finally, the cherry on the cake of this book is the *Dos* and *Don'ts*, which you'll find in every category and these should become your mantra when designing and developing, as they will tell you what you should and shouldn't do. By following the advice of people who have gained worldwide recognition for their work, you too could soon start to see your client base growing and some industry awards for your new-found creativity.

Rob Ford
Favourite Website Awards

Bio.
Rob Ford
Favourite Website Awards

Robert James Ford is FWA's
Founder and Principal. Born
and bred in England with a
background in finance, sales
and project management,
Rob has worked for
companies like Halifax Plc
and American Express. He
oversees the day-to-day
running of the FWA project.

Rob has pre-screened every
site that has ever been
submitted to FWA since
2000, which must be in the
region of over two hundred
thousand websites. He also
writes and contributes to
numerous other publications,
both online and offline, and
has judged for a number of
web award shows, as well as
having his work recognised
internationally.
–
www.thefwa.com

Do
Read
this
book

Don't
Let it
collect
dust

Interface & Design

Interface &
Design

Introduction by
Michael Lebowitz, Big Spaceship

01

Interface
Design

Interface

An explosion in broadband connectivity and the maturation of tools and platforms over the last several years has radically shifted the terrain of design for the web. It has evolved beyond its origins as a medium best suited to information delivery into a rich ecosystem of interdisciplinary influences: film, television, video games, animation, music composition, software, commerce, information, architecture, and editorial design, to name only the most prominent. The introduction of Flash video has sparked a revolution in video use, which we've barely begun to tap, that enables emotion and experience to take up their rightful place on the web alongside information and data.

"The technology evolves at a dizzying clip. Best practices are constantly being promulgated and then revised. The one constant is change."

Interactive design presents unforeseen challenges and opportunities that require us to step outside some of our comfort zones. We can't fall back on the long-established print tradition. Designing for a printed page, though by no means simple, has long-established foundations to build on, and changes in the medium are nuanced. (Papers and inks have evolved, typefaces have multiplied, but the enterprise remains the same.) And once you print it… it's printed. The interactive designer, by contrast, must consider, at least at present, end-user differences in bandwidth, screen resolution, and processor speed. (How would it have affected early filmmakers if their films couldn't be counted on to play at 24 frames per second, but rather played 24 in some theatres and 18 in others?) And those are just some of the technical challenges. Designing for the web calls for the typographic sensibilities of print, the ability to convey meaning over time of animation, film and video, and the grasp of interaction and human factors of application and game design.

The existence of a user changes everything. In print, you know your reader is flipping the pages left to right (or right to left, depending on where you live.) But in the web you can't prescribe how people use what you've made – only offer suggestions. As a result, the interactive designer is responsible for an ongoing dialog.

Over the past ten years, as the web has propagated among homes and schools across the country, people have become a lot more familiar with user interface and web architecture. A truly unique great website should surprise their expectations without confusing them; the interface should be, in the mode of the classic English butler, a helpful guide but never an intrusive presence.

The technology evolves at a dizzying clip. Best practices are constantly being promulgated and then revised. The one constant is change. With a canvas that can accommodate so many forms, and so many variables in the end-user experience, beginning any interactive project can feel like a step into the great unknown. At Big Spaceship, we focus by first asking ourselves basic questions about our audience and their experience:

Audience
– Who is this for?

Site Function
– What does it do for the audience?

Interaction
– What story are we trying to tell?
– What conversation are we trying to start?

Our answers to these questions become the basis of our understanding of every project we do, regardless of the client or the brand. It's very important that technological limitations don't enter into the equation until we have a solid understanding of the underlying conversation. Technology is the means of delivery, the enabler of function, but it provides little value without a vibrant underlying concept.

"With a canvas that can accommodate so many forms, and so many variables in the end-user experience, beginning any interactive project can feel like a step into the great unknown."

Our site for Nike Air *(see chapter 5, category: Showreels & Motion Graphics)* is an example of using technology in the service of narrative. When we were brainstorming for our initial pitch, no one mentioned feasibility. We only talked about our audience and what would engage them (and us). We wanted our users to experience the sensation of running on air, not just of watching it.

As we discussed our rough concepts internally and then with the Nike team, the project started to take shape. We began exploring our ideas more concretely, visually. What we wanted to do was ambitious, but we were still unwilling to rein it in it for technical reasons. We built a prototype, and in the course of doing so created the tools that would enable the experience we wanted the audience to have. This is one of the most important differentiating aspects of interactive design.

Part of our design process is creating tools that work in the service of the ultimate goals of the project. This is a process that programmers are intimately familiar with, a programming language is a way of describing function, but it doesn't provide function in and of itself. In other words, because what we make does things, we need to manipulate technology to make it do what we want. It is the combined creative disciplines of design and function, working in tandem, that lead to good work. Our fantastical ideas began to come down to earth of their own accord, but only where they had to. Our willingness to experiment had fruitful results.

There's an important lesson there: it's far easier to edit your ideas down to make them functional than to shoehorn an idea into an existing functionality. If you brew your coffee too strong, you can always add water, but weak coffee remains sad and undrinkable.

The sheer magnitude of experimentation and the creation of new functionality that accommodates storytelling (think YouTube, among others) can be attributed to the rapid development cycles and ease of publishing that characterize the web. We can be grateful for and exploit this flexibility. It allows us to pursue tangents and build prototypes that would be too costly to attempt in other media.

The work included here represents multiple vectors of possibility in the current ecosystem of the web. They're exciting examples of the experimentation that is inherent to all the work being done (even and especially commercial work) in this evolving medium. But no matter how brilliant, the work that excited us two years ago has already been eclipsed by new and exciting projects that have taken advantage of the most current standards and technologies, and so it will remain for the foreseeable future, until, like print, we settle somewhat, into smaller nuanced changes.

For now, however, interactive design remains driven by experimentation and innovation. For us at Big Spaceship (and I would guess for all the people responsible for the work contained here) it's tremendously exciting to have a hand in, in some small way, the definition of something brand new.

Michael Lebowitz
Big Spaceship

Bio.
<u>Michael Lebowitz</u>
Big Spaceship

Michael Lebowitz is the Co-founder and CEO of Big Spaceship, a digital creative agency in Brooklyn, NY. Founded on the principals of collaboration, innovation and dedication to quality, Michael and Big Spaceship have garnered countless accolades including the highly coveted Cannes Lion, One Show, Clio, and Webby Awards.

He has lectured and led seminars internationally on design, entertainment and interactive marketing, and is a regular juror for many international creative awards. Michael has spoken at conferences and universities on emerging trends and technology including the Futures of Entertainment Conference at MIT and an annual seminar on digital marketing in Rome. He was recently named to the AIGA's Visionary Design Council.
–
www.bigspaceship.com

"The one constant is change."

Three Dimensional Computer Graphics is the art of creating a believable world. Objects have characteristics or properties such as shape, size, weight, orientation and colour. To make that world very realistic and also appealing, you need to set a rule and combine physics to create something that leaves a lasting impression.

Do

1
Remember that if you can see it, you should make it the absolute best it can be.

2
Bear in mind that what you create doesn't have to be 100% realistic but it has to be very believable.

3
Take people away to another place in their imaginations.

Don't

1
Get too carried away with your graphics.

2
Make your creations and 3D work too complicated.

3
Go into too much detail. Whilst detail can be great, spending far too much time on any particular detail can become counterproductive.

Expert information by
Go Takahashi, Heiwa Alpha Co.

Heiwa Alpha

Agency
Heiwa Alpha Co.

Designed/Developed by
Heiwa Alpha Co.

Software
Maya

Awards
FWA Site Of The Day

Launched
2006

Action City

Agency
GrupoW

Designed
Miguel Calderon

Developed by
Ulises Valencia,
Sebastian Mariscal,
Raul Uranga, Daniel Bates

Software
Flash, 3ds Max, After Effects

Awards
FWA Site Of The Day

Launched
2007

www.grupowprojects.com/
rexona

The New Carnival

Agency
Nutility

Designed/Developed by
Joon Yong Park,
Sung Ju Lee, Jae Hun Lee

Software
After Effects, 3ds Max, Flash

Awards
FWA Site Of The Day

Launched
2006

Colour is a form of communication. If you use it with love and care, colour can be one of your strongest weapons of communication. Colour can make people happy, sad or at its best, fall in love. It's a matter of precision. Think of colour as music... some songs are sad, some hard to describe and some can move mountains. Colour for websites is like music for films.

Visually, colour works in the same way in all media. Technically, what separates different colours are their codenames, RGB, CMYK, PANTONE, HEX (web).

Remember that the beholder of colour is the eyes and you can create memorable moments if you can make candy for them. There are no rules but to us less is more.

Do

1
Use colours that add something to your work and give the design the right balance.

2
Figure out what you want to say and then try to find the colour that matches your objectives best.

3
Get constant feedback from others and always work hard and explore different alternatives.

Don't

1
Use too many different colours as it's pretty easy to end up with colour-overkill.

2
Use the brightest colours to catch your audience's attention. It's much more effective if you can achieve balance and harmony.

3
Copy others — your work is much more valuable as the original.

Expert information by
Robert Lindström & Staffan Lamm, North Kingdom

Alsklingsmacka

Agency
Åkestam.Holst and
North Kingdom

Designed by
Åkestam.Holst and
North Kingdom

Developed by
North Kingdom

Software
Flash, Photoshop, Maya,
3ds Max, After Effects

Awards
FWA Site Of The Day

Launched
2006

http://dev2.northkingdom.
com/fjallbrynt

Morgonmacka

Fullscreen in web terms generally refers to the expansion of a website to fill the entire computer screen. It's now also commonly used to describe the use of large scale video and imagery within a website.

Fullscreen, when used properly can enhance an immersive experience by demanding the user's full attention. However, it can come off like a person with a siren on their head, shrieking at you with a bullhorn if used improperly. It's a decision that shouldn't be taken lightly.

Do

1
Create an experience worthy of the attention you're demanding.

2
Consider your audience and the purpose of the site before jumping into a fullscreen solution.

If Google and YouTube were fullscreen websites, you would have never heard of them.

3
Give the user the option to visit a non-fullscreen version of the website if possible.

Don't

1
Force scroll bars. Be conscious of your target's screen resolution.

2
Use fullscreen video just because you can. If you're forcing the user to suffer through painfully heavy load times, a smaller player is probably a good idea.

3
Compromise the integrity of video with compression If fullscreen video looks like crap after compressing it to an acceptable size, don't do it.

Expert information by
Will McGinness, Goodby, Silverstein & Partners

Comcastic

Agency
Goodby, Silverstein &
Partners, The Barbarian
Group, Natzke Design,
Branden Hall, number 9

Designed by
Will McGinness, Keith
Anderson, Toria Emery,
Toria Emery, Mike Geiger,
Amanda Kelso, Dora Lee,
Devin Sharkey, Brian Taylor

Developed by
The Barbarian Group,
Natzke Design, Branden
Hall, number 9, Keytoon
Animation Studio, Gino
Nave, Chris Ewen,
Sean Drinkwater

Software
Flash, Photoshop, Final Cut,
Illustrator, Maya 3D

Awards
FWA Site Of The Month,
FITC, One Show Bronze,
Cannes Cyber Lion Gold,
LIAA Gold

Launched
2005

The intro-sequence of a website can be a very helpful communication tool. It presents a company's core values in an entertaining way. It pulls people into new worlds. It builds up a positive image in a couple of seconds. It gives a warm welcome and a motivation to stay. It burns your message into people's minds. It makes visitors enter your website with a smile on their face.

Like a good movie trailer, it makes people curious and begging for more. Or, it simply scares everybody away — if not done well.

Do

1
Inform and entertain the viewer.

2
Respect bandwidth.

3
Provide a *Skip Intro* button.

Don't

1
Be boring — try and entertain.

2
Be ugly — be creative and make your intro visually pleasing.

3
Provide useless information.

Expert information by
Rainer Michael, WM Team

Intros

A6 Allroad Quattro

Agency
Saatchi & Saatchi
– Interactive (Frankfurt)

Designed by
Sascha Geier, Sascha Lee,
Christian Bartsch, Sebastian
Schier, Peter Huschka

Developed by
David Szakaly, Sascha
Geier, Alexander Valentin,
Martin Anderle, Wolfgang
Müller

Software
Photoshop, Flash, After
Effects, Final Cut Pro HD,
3ds Max

Awards
FWA Site Of The Day,
Golden Drum, Annual
Multimedia, Mobius Award

Launched
2006

http://microsites.audi.com/
campaigns/allroad_quattro

WM Team:
Showtime for your brand

Agency
WM Team GmbH

Designed by
Rainer Michael

Developed by
Jens Franke, Tobias
Schmalenbach

Software
Flash, FreeHand,
Photoshop, Audition 1.5

Awards
FWA Site Of The Day,
Ultrashock BombShock,
Mäx Site Of The Month

Launched
2006

www.wmteam.com

Junior's Giants

Agency
Funktion12 (RED Interactive
Agency)

Designed/Developed by
Jared Kroff

Software
Photoshop, Flash

Awards
FWA Site Of The Day

Launched
2005

www.juniorsgiants.com

The use of a metaphor for a site is about bringing people's offline sensibilities into the online world. Metaphors can bring interest and a known visual guide to a site's navigation. If the metaphor is taken throughout the site, it can also help to clearly delineate areas and bring direction to their content and dynamic motion.

The choice of metaphor is important however; if it is not directly linked to the product or service in question it serves to imbue the brand with certain values. The House of Naked for example, was about more than the clever use of a floor plan; it was about presenting a global family with different interests and skills all "living" in the same extraordinary house and who share a perspective on the world of communications.

Once seen as an evolution from brochure ware, metaphor driven websites have come of age as users demand rich online experiences with a sense of grounding.

Do

1
Use a metaphor if it helps a site's navigation.

Don't

2
Use a metaphor if it enhances the user's experience.

1
Stretch the metaphor too far.

3
Choose a metaphor that is appropriate for your brand and product/service.

2
Mix metaphors.

3
Hide behind the metaphor or let it become bigger than your brand and/or product/service.

Expert information by
Matt Hardisty, Naked Communications

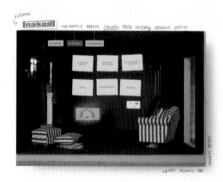

Naked

Agency
Hi-ReS!

Designed/Developed by
Hi-ReS!

Software
Flash

Awards
FWA Site Of The Day

Launched
2005

www.nakedcomms.com

Bobby Womack

Agency
sofake

Designed/Developed by
Jordan Stone

Software
Photoshop, Flash

Awards
FWA Site Of The Day

Launched
2003

www.archive.bobbywomack.
sofake.com

Concept M

Agency
Concept M

Designed by
Niek Bokkers

Developed by
Nico Stam

Software
Photoshop, Flash,
Deamweaver

Awards
FWA Site Of The Day

Launched
2006

www.conceptm.nl

Japanese people have always been good at minimal expression, as can be seen right back to ancient times. "Beauty born by subtraction" can be seen in many areas of Japanese culture, especially its fine arts and its architecture.

We are fascinated and thrilled by the beauty and depth which are born by subtraction rather than addition. We also think minimal expression is important especially in today's society because our modern world is surrounded by too much information and too much urgency.

Do

1
Be conscious of
visual expressions as
a language.

2
Consider other
communication tools
other than language
alone.

3
Show awareness in
the art of balancing all
aspects of your work.

Don't

1
Focus too heavily on
a minimal presence;
let your expression
come through.

2
Try and combine
too many different
elements at one time.

3
Take on a project that
you are not focused
on fulfilling.

Expert information by
Shun Kawakami, artless Inc.

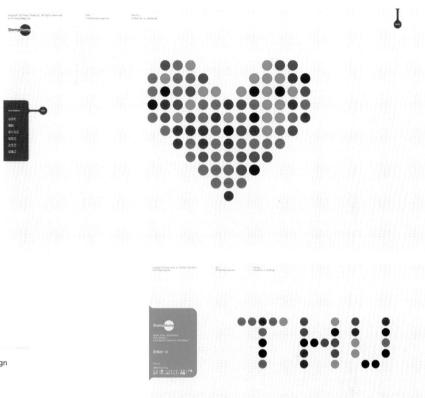

Stomp Stamp

Agency
artless and .sfpdesign

Designed by
Yu-ki Sakurai

Developed by
Takashi Kamada

Software
Illustrator, Photoshop, Flash

Awards
FWA Site Of The Day,
Adobe Motion Award

Launched
2006

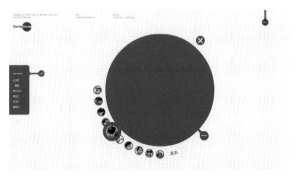

35

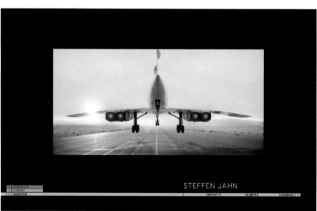

Steffen Jahn

Agency
Robinizer

Designed by
Wolfgang von Geramb

Developed by
Martin Schoberer

Software
Flash

Awards
FWA Site Of The Day,
iF Communication Award,
ITA

Launched
2005

www.steffenjahn.com

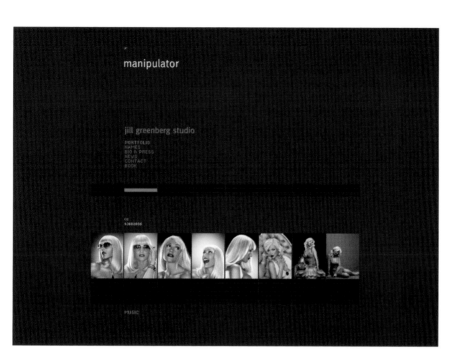

Manipulator

Agency
group94

Designed/Developed by
group94

Software
FreeHand, Illustrator, Flash,
Photoshop, PHP, MySQL

Awards
FWA Site Of The Day

Launched
2005

http://archive.group94.com/
manipulator

Less than a decade ago it was quite easy for a web designer to get his audience overwhelmed with a few simple *mouseover* effects on his menu items. Some JavaScript usually did the trick.

Those glorious days of early web-witchcraft are over since Flash entered the game. Nowadays a wide variety of visual effects can be achieved by means of timeline animations and programmed transitions, even including audio and video. Smart mathematics allows us to create extremely complex navigational systems. There are hardly any technical boundaries. The only limitation is the web designer's own imagination.

Do

1
Be creative, yet keep in mind that the main purpose of a menu is to navigate through a website. Your audience should immediately understand it's purpose and it's working.

2
Make sure that your navigation system is bullet proof.

3
Make sure, for instance, that the selected menu item is not clickable. Reloading the actual page because of a selected menu item still being clickable is the dumbest yet most common mistake.

Don't

1
Use that 10 year old JavaScript effect anymore, even if Jacob Nielsen says that you shouldn't use Flash.

2
Overestimate your audience either. Today's website visitor has little time and patience.

3
Forget that your user doesn't want to spend the rest of the day navigating through your website.

Expert information by
Pascal Leroy, group94

Navigation — Animated Menus

adidas Sport Style Y-3
Cubes

Agency
Neue Digitale

Designed/Developed by
Jörg Waldschütz, Jens
Steffen

Software
Flash, 3ds Max, Photoshop

Awards
FWA Site Of The Day, red
dot, Annual Multimedia
Award, Cresta, iF, New
York Festival, Deutscher
Multimedia Award, Cannes,
One Show, Clio, Montreux,
Andy, Vidfest, ADC
Deutschland, Eurobest,
Epica

Launched
2005

www.neue-digitale.de/
projects/y-3_fw2005

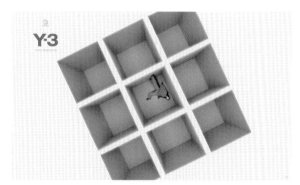

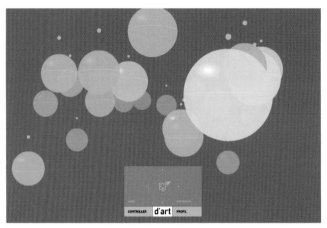

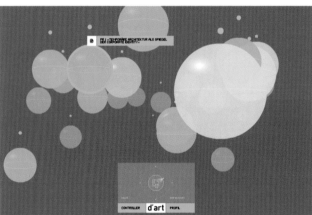

D'Art Design Gruppe

Agency
group94

Designed/Developed by
group94

Software
FreeHand, Flash,
Photoshop, TopStyle, Final
Cut Pro, PHP, MySQL

Awards
FWA Site Of The Day

Launched
2004

www.d-artdesign.de

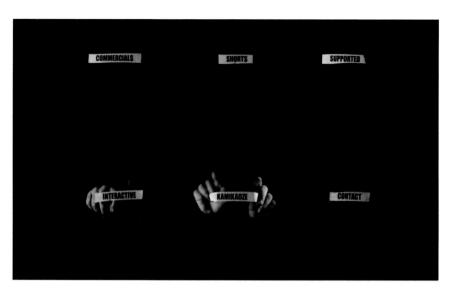

Kamikadze

Agency
Kamikadze S.R.O.

Designed/Developed by
Brano Pepel, Vilo Csino

Software
Flash, After Effects

Awards
FWA Site Of The Day,
Golden Nail Slovakia

Launched
2005

www.kamikadze.sk

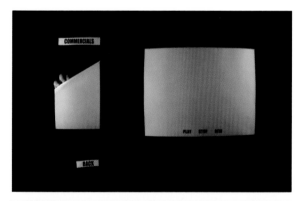

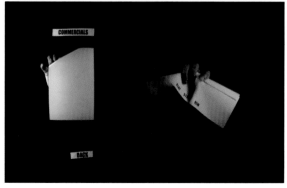

Hidden menus are desirable for their elegance and efficient use of space, focusing attention away from the navigation options, and onto the main stage. This is particularly helpful when viewing portfolios, reading long copy on a page, or simply cleaning up a dense navigation.

The key is to always have the hidden information easily accessible — it should never be a game of hide and seek. As the page builds, consider a brief animation where the soon-to-be-hidden menu reveals itself before minimizing to orient users.

Do

1
Be consistent. Use of the same color, action and motion for similar functionality helps users grasp your navigation easily.

2
Have the menu accessible at times, in all sections of the site.

3
Anticipate the user's needs and be sure to include intuitive links and multiple ways of arriving at the same place.

Don't

1
Reinvent the wheel. There are conventions already out there. Use them in new and interesting ways.

2
Try this for a non-savvy web audience. Hidden navigation is best suited for advanced users looking for a new experience.

3
Launch your site without conducting tests or focus groups with samples of the target audience. Fresh eyes on a project always help.

Expert information by
Marc S Levitt & Sheri L Koetting, MSLK

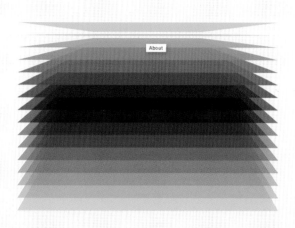

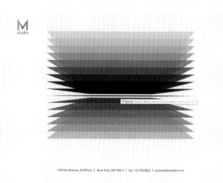

M Studio

Agency
MSLK

Designed
Marc S Levitt and
Sheri L Koetting

Developed by
Alex Motzenbecke

Software
Illustrator, Flash

Awards
FWA Site Of The Day

Launched
2006

www.mstudio.com

Navigation can singularly make or break a site. It is responsible for the enjoyment (and success) of the user's interaction; if they enjoy using it they will keep coming back. If they don't, you will never see them again. It should form the backbone to any content-rich site and the starting point for the organisation and architecture of your build.

Traditionally, navigation has always been entirely visible, giving the user the full range of options on screen at any one time. Horizontal navigation pushes its inherent purpose towards an explorative experience and it is during this exploration that you can surprise and delight the user and deliver content in an unexpected and enchanting way!

Do

1
Include "quick" navigation. Providing two alternate routes to important content will cater for two distinct types of user. This is particularly important when building explorative navigation.

2
Surprise your user! When breaking conventions make sure you have fun with it!

3
Apply some basic techniques — Parallax and depth of field can lift a flat 2D plane whilst Inertia adds fluidity to navigating.

Don't

1
Overload the computer! Pay careful attention to the total scrollable area and be mindful of how much the CPU has to move around the screen.

2
Ignore your user. Make sure the navigation is suited to the information you are delivering. A great explorative navigation system is not always the best way to deliver large amounts of information-heavy content.

3
Develop another 2D town-scope. They have been done to death!

Expert information by
Phil Stuart, Preloaded

Carlos Polo

Agency
Carlos Polo Araújo

Designed/Developed by
Carlos Polo Araújo

Software
Flash, Photoshop

Awards
FWA Site Of The Day

Launched
2006

www.carlos-polo.com/
index_old.html

SectionSeven Inc.

Agency
SectionSeven Inc

Designed
Craig Erickson

Developed by
Jason Keimig

Software
Illustrator, Photoshop, Flash

Awards
FWA Site Of The Day

Launched
2006

www.sectionseven.com/
index2.html

Tongsville

Agency
Preloaded

Designed/Developed by
Preloaded

Software
Photoshop, Flash

Awards
FWA Site Of The Month,
SXSW Winner Best Film
Industry Site, SXSW Winner
Best of Show, BAFTA
Finalist, BIMA Finalist, Flash
In The Can Finalist, IVCA
Finalist, Ultrashock Shocked
Site, Macromedia Showcase

Launched
2001

www.tongsville.com/city

Being one of the most common and ancient navigation types in the existence of the World Wide Web, one might overlook the potential elegance, effectiveness and impact of vertical navigation.

Redefined in the current age of the Internet vertical navigations are now accessible and super-sexy at the same time. If designed with the right shape, behaviour dynamics and filled with the right content, vertical navigation may result in significantly enhanced user interaction and exceptional user experience.

Do

1
Balance play and function. If balanced the right way vertical navigation becomes part of your story or identity.

2
Treat navigation as content. Make the journey to the content at least as important as the content itself.

3
Make it snappy and ensure the user feels in control.

Don't

1
Exaggerate navigation transitions.

2
Hide your navigation.

3
Annoy the user with your newly discovered tricks and if you do, make sure it adds to the usability and the experience.

Expert information by
Remon Tijssen, Fluid

Bascule Inc.

Agency
Bascule Inc

Designed
Mitsuhiro Oga

Developed by
Nobuo Hara, Kampei Baba,
Go Kameda

Software
Flash

Awards
FWA Site Of The Day,
D&AD Awards 2006 Yellow
Pencil, Cannes Cyber Lions
2006 Shortlist, One Show
Interactive 2006 Finalist,
Clio Awards 2006 Shortlist,
Asia Pacific Advertising
Festival 2006 Gold, The
4th Tokyo Interactive Ad
Awards Website Corporate
Site Silver

Launched
2005

www.bascule.co.jp

Fluid

Agency
Fluid

Designed/Developed by
Remon Tijssen

Software
Flash

Awards
FWA Site Of The Day

Launched
2005

www.fluid.nl

JBL – Destination
Anywhere Tour

Agency
Firstborn

Designed/Developed by
Firstborn

Software
Flash, XML, PHP, 3ds Max

Awards
FWA Site Of The Day

Launched
2006

www.fborn.com/
websites/137_jbl

51

The navigation of a site is one of the most important elements to consider in the creative process, especially if the site does not use what could be termed as "conventional" navigation. Usability and functionality have to be taken into account at the time of concept.

In order to obtain successful navigation it is necessary to consider at least two levels of structure:

Logic structure
The general structure of the site, where the topics and subtopics are shown in a hierarchical way as well as all the possible ways to cross-navigate within the website.

Visual structure (or layout of the interface)
In this stage are planned menus, windows, buttons, tools, etc.

Beyond this, it is worth adding the surprise factor, which can enhance a user's experience and give them an unforgettable moment. A site with creative navigation can make a huge difference and can help to spread a website's address globally by the viral "word of mouth" effect.

Do

1
Allow users to know where they are at all times within a website.

2
Create navigation systems that are simple to use and understand.

3
Consider using navigation that surprises and creates an unforgettable moment.

Don't

1
Build confusing navigation that makes the user lose his or her place in a website.

2
Create navigation that takes up too much space and makes content become secondary.

3
Create navigation that changes it's logical use at any time.

Expert information by
Miguel Calderón, GrupoW

Saab Saibu Tour

Agency
Bascule Inc.

Designed
Yusuke Kitani, Yuko
Tomioka

Developed by
Nobuo Hara, Kampei Baba

Software
Flash

Awards
FWA Site Of The Day

Launched
2005

http://awards.bascule.co.jp/
2006/saab/en

Semillero

Agency
GrupoW

Designed
Miguel Calderon, Cesar
Morenoe

Developed by
Ulises Valencia, Sebastian
Mariscal, Raul Uranga

Software
Flash, Fractal Painter

Awards
FWA Site Of The Day, El Sol
from San Sebastian Bronze,
Ojo de Iberoamerica
Bronze, ITA Site Of The
Month, Círculo Creativo
Gold, a!Diseño Best Website

Launched
2006

www.semillero.net

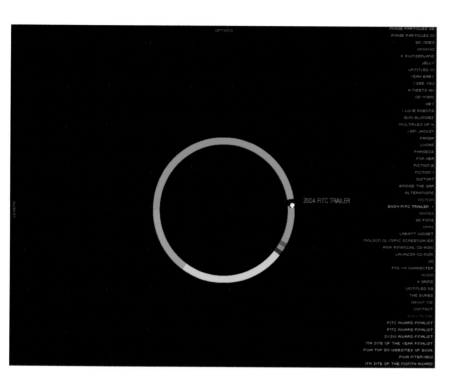

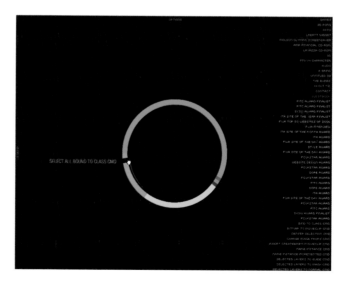

Self Titled

Agency
John Iacoviello

Designed/Developed by
John Iacoviello

Software
Flash, SEPY ActionScript
Editor

Awards
FWA Site Of The Day,
ITA Site Of The Month

Launched
2006

www.selftitled.ca

A classic question when creating websites is, to use a pop-up or not! The main question is: Do we have to choose between a fullscreen or pop-up experience, or make sure the classic browser tools are accessible in the browser? Launching a site in fullscreen or a fixed size pop up allows you to get the user's full attention and focus, which is ideal for full-on multimedia experiences.

On the other hand, the classic browser page is more ergonomic and useful for watching editorial content. You have all your usual tools to hand, and you can easily bookmark, print or move to another website quickly.

The best practice concerning this is to develop several versions and give your users the choice when they enter your site.

Do

1
Have a visible *Close* button to quit fullscreen or close a site launched in a fixed size pop-up.

2
Use a script that will allow your pop-up to open if the user has a pop-up blocker activated in their browser.

3
Insert simple buttons to allow users to bookmark or print content.

Don't

1
Forget to let users know they are about to launch a pop-up or fullscreen website.

2
Hesitate to make a page underneath the pop-up or fullscreen site to possibly display a product or logo and this is also a good chance to thank your users for visiting.

3
Forget that the over use and abuse of pop-ups inside your website can cause some of your content to be hidden, as well as annoying your users.

Expert information by
Olivier Marchand & Benjamin Laugel, Soleil Noir

iam studios

Agency
Fat-Man Collective
(+ Vortice Studios)

Designed/Developed by
David Okuniev

Software
Flash, 3ds Max

Awards
FWA Site Of The Day

Launched
2007

www.iam-studios.nl

As with any design project, typography plays a vital role in successfully communicating your ideas. Refer to your client's Corporate Identity or Brand Guidelines — very often a pre-selected typeface at a range of different weights and point sizes will have been defined in order to maintain the integrity of the brand.

In the case where no brand guidelines have been specified, a wider range of typefaces can be explored. For example, sometimes a highly stylized typeface when used in moderation can enrich and complement the elements within a layout.

Do

1
Ensure that main site navigation is clear and legible.

2
Define links clearly on a page, this can be achieved with an accent color, weight, or variation in point size.

3
Layout footer information using a typeface that is clear and legible at small point sizes.

Don't

1
Use overly stylized typefaces when laying out large amounts of body copy.

2
Mix a wide variety of typefaces on a page.

3
Offset Flash bitmap typefaces, this will result in blurring.

Expert information by
John White, Firstborn

OurType

Agency
group94

Designed/Developed by
group94

Software
FreeHand, Flash, PHP, MySQL

Awards
FWA Site Of The Day

Launched
2004

www.ourtype.be

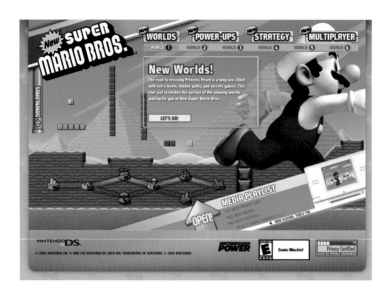

Agency
Pop

Designed
Joel Eby

Developed by
Dave Curry

Software
Photoshop, Flash

Awards
FWA Site Of The Day,
Adobe Site Of The Day,
American Design Awards

Launched
2006

http://mario.nintendo.com

cmd9

Agency
cmd9

Designed/Developed by
Junichi Kato

Software
Flash

Awards
FWA Site Of The Day

Launched
2006

http://cmd9.com

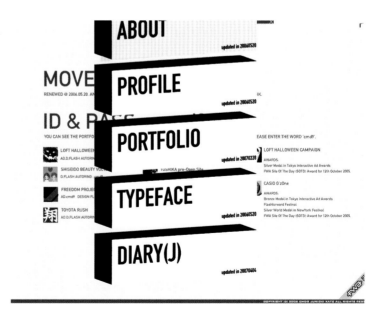

firstborn

OUR PORTFOLIO
WHO WE ARE
WHAT WE DO
WHY US
OUR NEWS **THE DIFFERENCE**
CONTACT US

DESIGN

Firstborn is determined to make sure the image on the computer screen mirrors the image our clients have supplied to us. In fact, we try to make the image look even better. Whether it's a photo from an advertising campaign or picture of a specific model, a company logo or corporate collateral, Firstborn treats each and every image as we would our own. We take great care to preserve the integrity of all images supplied by our clients. We crop, scan, digitally enhance and even shoot the pictures ourselves to make sure all images are presented in the best possible light. And even though we specialize in the digital medium, we are first and foremost designers. Firstborn produces numerous print projects for both established brands and new products in need of branding.

Whatever the project may be, Firstborn always attempts to create the most memorable designs possible. If audiences don't have a recollection of the work we produced, then we did not do our jobs right.

MANAGEMENT
PROJECT BIDDING
DELIVERY

THE RECOGNITION

firstborn

OUR PORTFOLIO
WHO WE ARE
WHAT WE DO
WHY US
OUR NEWS
CONTACT US

DESIGN PHILOSOPHY

There are key principles that shape our design philosophy. Keep things simple. Hide elements, but leave them accessible. Subtract, allowing the most important elements to rise to the surface. These mantras apply equally to both traditional and interactive design.

We study and follow the best examples of contemporary graphic design and typography. We read books on geometry, physics and trigonometry, and we apply our knowledge to interactive design. We keep our finger on the pulse of whats new, different and engaging in print design. This results in simple yet sophisticated user experiences and campaigns that we, and our clients, are very proud of.

We believe that what is happening in interactive design now is similar to the graphic design revolution of the past. We maintain good relations with many leading graphic designers and feel that exchanging ideas leads to the further development of our trade.

BUSINESS PHILOSOPHY
HISTORY

Firstborn

Agency
Firstborn

Designed
Vas Sloutchevsky

Developed by
Gicheol Lee

Software
Photoshop, Flash, .NET, XML

Awards
FWA Site Of The Day,
Communication Arts,
Macromedia Site Of The Day

Launched
2002 then 2006

www.fborn.com/#/our-portfolio/505/screenshots

61

Marketing & Communication

Introduction by
Martin Hughes & Jordan Stone, WEFAIL

02

When we were first approached to write this chapter intro on successful campaigns I thought — "Why us?" But as the sun came up over Mulholland's Hills and made the Pacific Ocean glisten in its rays, I sat and looked out at our beautiful estate overlooking PCH101. Jordan was out front on the main lawn hosing down the geraniums, he looks so tanned now, his muscular shoulders sun kissed and golden, then the answer came to me — "Well, who else could write it?" You see from day one success has followed WEFAIL like a curious happy cat, rubbing around our legs and purring its financial goodness all around us. How do WEFAIL keep the cat of success content? We shall explain.

> **"Do it your way, it may not work, people may laugh at your crappy idea, but at least you haven't spent your time trying to copy some other studio like a big trend whore."**

Always feed the cat 100% dopeness
A successful campaign isn't made by ten Ad Agency people blabbering away in an office and then telling you how to design. A successful campaign isn't made by a hands on client that wants to take your ideas and rub them around in poop. A successful campaign isn't guaranteed because it's for a big brand client riding it into glory (for even the biggest clients are capable of making a giant steaming turd of a website). No, success comes from you doing what you do best so don't let them take away your music!!!

Don't design what Donny Don't does
For God's sake, don't copy other designers… is it really so hard to walk away from the computer and think of an original idea? No it's not, unless you're not very good and in that case copy! The biggest part of making a successful, popular site is to be original. Do it your way, it may not work, people may laugh at your crappy idea, but at least you haven't spent your time trying to copy some other studio like a big trend whore. Why can't you just be happy in your own brilliant mind?

Summon the mighty power of Thronodon
An ancient wise master at the gates of oblivion once told us: "If you're going to rock, rock it hard and true." It made me cry.

Technology is a dangerous tool

If you ask me, a super fantastic Flash site doesn't have to use every tool in the box. It may only use one, say for instance tweens! Just because you have the tools to add a thousand new effects doesn't mean you need to use them. I for one am sick of seeing Alpha Video super slick web commercials that are supposedly interactive yet leave the user very little to actually do… apart from sit and watch it play. In that example the tool has become more important than the concept… and that sucks. You must be a Flash assassin, armed only with a crappy knife… but have the ability to get in close with your awesome idea and kill for success!!!

"Do not under any circumstances spend four weeks storyboarding an idea and making such a rigid work plan that the whole site becomes some stiff over-planned piece of poo."

Don't think too hard

You know, some of the best ideas are easy. Don't overcook it, do not under any circumstances spend four weeks storyboarding an idea and making such a rigid work plan that the whole site becomes some stiff over-planned piece of poo. Some of the biggest studios in the world do this and it sucks. You can suffocate your very creativity by planning too much. But these big studios pay by the hour so the art directors like to play around with glitter and kid's poster paints on big stupid A1 cards which all results in horrid post grad looking BS. Just let it happen! Let the ideas fall out as you go along, naturally.

Short people can't jump (or design*)

I know it sounds ludicrous but it's so true. You see short people are by their very nature… angry. They have a lot of built up frustration and it all comes out in their work. If you're male and below 5'8", give up now or else face a life of utter fury, bitterness and Cuban heels.

*If you're female and short this rule does not apply as short girls are cute and usually happy beings.

Two words: Be confident!

That's right, be confident about your work. If you believe in your
work — that will make them (the enemy, the client… a necessary
evil) believe in you. If you show an ounce of doubt about your work
then they will leverage that doubt into a whole Pandora's Box of
problems by jumping in with both feet and telling you how to design
the site. "I always liked the colour red. Can you make the site red?
And make the text bounce like its dancing?" No! You see, every
client wants to be a designer but nature never blesses one person
with both artistic skills and the gift of spewing forth utter BS and
lies. Make sure they don't cross the line… be strong! For you are
the giant key to your own success!

Now go forth and unlock your amazing potential!

Martin Hughes and Jordan Stone
WEFAIL

Bio.
Martin Hughes
& Jordan Stone
WEFAIL

WEFAIL are Martin Hughes and
Jordan Stone, formed in 2003
these two dandy Flash warriors
have gone on to slay such
fearsome dragons as Eminem,
The Dixie Chicks, BBDO, MTV,
Billy Harvey, Bob Schneider,
and many more beastly foes.

They have won many awards
in their short stumpy lives
including the musician category
of SXSW every year for more
years than they can remember.
–
www.wefail.com

"Always feed the cat 100% dopeness."

Providing your company's contact details is possibly the most important section of your website. It is essential that your contact information is easily found on your website with the obvious *Contact* link, visible at all times.

Simple, concise and easy to understand information on your "Contact" page is vitally important, whilst going the extra mile and providing different language versions for foreign visitors, as well as items like travel information (by train, parking, from the airport etc.), and a print-friendly map of how to find you will impress those who visit your site.

Do	Don't
1 Clearly display a *Contact* link at all times.	**1** Make it hard to find your contact details.
2 Provide an email-direct option and contact form as an alternative for those without direct access to an email client.	**2** Offer too many contact choices that will confuse the user.
3 Clearly display your company address and telephone number complete with the international dialling code.	**3** Offer only a *Click Here* button without displaying the email address.

Expert information by
Chris Sees, Square Circle Media

Soleil Noir

Agency
Soleil Noir

Designed by
Alex Tyack

Developed by
Morgane Peinado

Software
Flash, Photoshop, Illustrator

Awards
FWA Site Of The Day,
ITA Site Of The Month,
Macromedia Site Of The
Week

Launched
2004

Square Circle

Agency
Square Circle Media

Designed by
Daniel Burnside

Developed by
George Medve and
Chris Sees

Software
Eclipse, FDT, PHPeclipse,
Flash, After Effects, Creative
Suite, Cinema 4D

Awards
FWA Site Of The Day, ITA

Launched
2006

www.sqcircle.com

02 Marketing & Communication

WDDG

Agency
WDDG

Designed by
George Ernst

Developed by
Constantin Koumouzelis

Software
After Effects, Final Cut,
Flash, Photoshop, Illustrator

Awards
FWA Site Of The Day

Launched
2006

www.wddg.com

mediaBOOM

Agency
mediaBOOM

Designed/Developed by
mediaBOOM

Software
Flash

Awards
FWA Site of the Day,
Webby Award, Pixel Awards,
American Design Awards,
Web Design International
Festival, W3 Awards

Launched
2005

www.mediaboom.com

It is essential to tell the story behind your organisation's history, capabilities, and goals. Illustrating who you are through text, images, and even video helps visitors better understand what you are all about. The idea is to briefly communicate your competence, passion, or whatever other traits set you apart from the competition.

This section does not need to be lengthy or highly detailed. Visitors tend not to read exceedingly long pages of information, and will often skip over an entire section that is too wordy. A clear and focused message that quickly captures the attention of the reader will suffice.

Do

1
Explain how your organization came to be, the goals of your business, and what sets you apart from other companies.

Don't

2
Include images, video, or any other media that helps illustrate who you are.

1
Write so much content that the visitor skips over the section entirely.

3
Be brief and attempt to capture the visitor's attention in the shortest amount of time possible.

2
Overwhelm the reader with marketing speak or industry jargon that they may not understand or be turned off by.

3
Fail to explain what makes your company special.

Expert information by
Eric Jordan, 2Advanced Studios

2Advanced Studios
– About us

Agency
2Advanced Studios

Designed by
Eric Jordan, Shane Mielke,
Jonathan Moore, Baz Pringle

Developed by
Brad Jackson, Ryan Serra,
Sonny Kotler

Software
Flash, Photoshop,
After Effects, Maya,
Dreamweaver, Go Live,
Illustrator, Cinema 4D

Awards
FWA Site of the Day, Adobe
Site of the Week, Ultrashock
Bombshock, Web Marketing
Association's WebAward
Interactive, W3 Award Best
in Show

Launched
2006

www.2advanced.com/
#company/about

73

Websites these days are becoming more and more visual. We're doing things that were unthinkable a couple of years ago. Today we can do 35 mm film productions that are solely made for the interactive world. This is just incredible, but it also presents new challenges.

We all know that we are watching an illusion, so we have to make the viewer believe what they are watching. The audience has to make a pact with itself to decide that they want to buy into the story and that they want to interact and therefore go further into the site.

In the Saab *Animal Vision* example you have to believe that we are in a Swedish forest in the middle of the winter (which we are not). You have to believe that we are watching the car from the eyes of an animal (which, surprise, we are not). If you can make them believe all of this you have created the right atmosphere.

Do

1
Build it up. Let the user get a feel for the world you want to create in his or her head.

2
Lure them in. The viewer wants to discover the site bit by bit.

Just as you unfold the story of a Hollywood movie to the audience, throw some bones at the visitor along the way to make them want to see more and click through your site.

3
Go for quality.

Don't

1
Be too obvious. Many people (you know who you are) want websites to be foolproof. They want instructions, arrows and *"cliquez ici"* all over the place.

2
Forget the sound. Sound plays a big part in making the atmosphere.

3
Forget that interaction, atmosphere and originality is the key to a successful campaign.

Expert information by
Johan Tesch, Lowe Tesch

Saab Animal Vision

Agency
Lowe Tesch

Designed by
Tim Scheiel

Developed by
Daniel Isaksson

Software
Flash

Awards
FWA Site Of The Month,
Creative Review, One Show,
New York Festivals, Epica

Launched
2006

Oculart

Agency
Geoff Lillemon

Designed/Developed by
Geoff Lillemon

Software
Photoshop, After Effects,
Illustrator,

Awards
FWA Site Of The Day,
Flash Forward Art

Launched
2000

www.oculart.com

Lana Landis

Agency
247 MediaStudios

Designed/Developed by
Ingo J. Ramin

Software
Photoshop, Flash, CoolEdit
Pro

Awards
FWA Site Of The Day

Launched
2003

www.lanalandis.com

Mindflood

Agency
Mindflood

Designed by
Chris Lund, Mike Hansen,
Noah Costello

Developed by
Chris Kief

Software
Flash, After Effects,
Photoshop

Awards
FWA Site Of The Day

Launched
2006

www.mindflood.com

Surprise is the basic emotive response to the unexpected. Surprise can be found in humour, subtle detail, the odd, and the extraordinary. It is an element that is often over utilised in the broadcast medium and underutilised in the interactive medium.

Creating the reaction of genuine surprise in a user enhances all aspects of the experience. We often refer to this as "layers of discovery"; hence, the more layers, the more depth a site has, the greater the result.

Do

1
Look for opportunities to create the unexpected. The element of surprise acts like the hook on a piece of music — if successful, it fixates the consumer.

2
Sweat the details. If you can add surprise through a rollover, sound effect, or motion — do it. It is in this minutia that one gains the richness of a great experience.

3
Keep it simple. An engaging site is one that can be understood.

Don't

1
Overlook the end user. This is a common mistake. Know your target market and design for them.

2
Design in a bubble. Realize that what may be surprising to one culture might be old hat to another. If your marketplace is international take this into consideration.

3
Try too hard. Savvy consumers will be put off.

Expert information by
Michael Kern, Struck Design

Toyota – AYGO

Agency
North Kingdom

Designed by
Bjarne Melin

Developed by
Isak Wiström

Software
Flash, Photoshop

Awards
FWA Site Of The Day,
One Show Finalist, Clio
Awards Finalist, London
International Awards Finalist

Launched
2005

www.northkingdom.com/
competition/aygo/en

Philips Bodygroom

Agency
Tribal DDB New York and
Struck Design

Designed by
Tribal DDB New York

Developed by
Struck Design

Software
Illustrator, Photoshop, Flash,
On2 Flix

Awards
FWA Site Of The Year, FWA
Site Of The Month, New
York Festivals, London
International Award, Cannes
Lion Gold, Communication
Arts, Adage, Business Week,
Adweek, Wall Street Journal

Launched
2006

IKEA – Dream Kitchen

Agency
Forsman & Bodenfors

Designed by
Forsman & Bodenfors

Developed by
Forsman & Bodenfors,

Production
Kokokaka, Stop, Syndicate

Software
Adobe CS, After Effects,
Flash, Inferno

Awards
FWA Site Of The Day,
Cannes, Epica, Eurobest,
New York Festivals, One
Show, LIA, Campaign Digital
Awards, Flash Forward,
D&AD, Clio Awards, ADC
New York, Guldägget

Launched
2006

http://demo.fb.se/e/ikea/
dreamkitchen2/site/
default.html

The traditional ways of entertainment have always been one-way communication between the writer/reader, singer/spectator or actor/audience for a long time. The power of the Internet is the instant two-way communication it provides and also the fastest means of feedback.

We still feel the joy of listening to music or watching a movie but channels like online gaming and creative user interfaces have created a large open playing field for all types of new entertainment.

The possibilities of user-created content and the ability to fulfil the needs and senses of touching, changing, creating, improving or destroying content has never been greater.

Do

1
Focus on the idea and try it on yourself. If you don't think it is fun, it probably isn't.

2
Let the user interact, create something, change something or at least touch or press something. A simple play bar is better than a self-playing movie.

3
Make it easy to give feedback, not only for your visitors, but also for yourself. Feedback makes your application or game better.

Don't

1
Underestimate the user. They want to have fun and they will learn how to use your navigation.

2
Always believe your site needs a story. If you're not a storyteller or comedian, do something else. Create a feature that allows users to make their own content or create a game.

3
Make your idea too big or too long. Short great ideas can be as entertaining as a three-hour movie.

Expert information by
Tony Högqvist, Perfect Fools

The Bar

Agency
Arc Worldwide

Designed/Developed by
Arc Worldwide

Software
Flash

Awards
FWA Site Of The Day,
WebAwards Outstanding
Website

Launched
2005

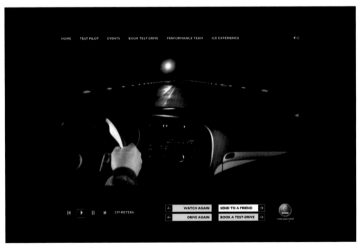

Saab Pilots Wanted

Agency
Lowe Tesch

Designed by
Tim Scheibel

Developed by
Perfect Fools

Software
Flash

Awards
FWA Site Of The Day, Epica

Launched
2006

http://dyc.saab-web.com/
microsites/pilotswanted/
GLOBAL/en/index2.shtml

Sprite Test Laboratories

Agency
Mortierbrigade

Designed/Developed by
group94

Software
Illustrator, Flash, Photoshop,
After Effects, 3ds Max, Final
Cut Pro, PHP, MySQL

Awards
FWA Site Of The Day

Launched
2006

http://archive.
mortierbrigade.com/
sprite3g/

Is there such a thing? When WEFAIL was first approached by Christian Aid to do a "good cause" site we thought, "oh no... does this mean we won't be getting paid? We like charities and such, but we like money better... how do we ask them? How awkward! Let's just ignore the email!"

But as it turned out they mentioned the issue of a fee before we had to bring it up and after that point WEFAIL were all about "charity"... we were just like Bono Theresa.

We built mailorderchickens.org in two months.

Do

1
Get 50% up front. I don't care if it's for a charity. Give me my 50% or I'm doing nothing!

2
Actually think about what the job aims to do. Plan out how you'll walk the user through the plight of the said charity and explain to them clearly how they can help.

3
Quickly pick out the key people you need to work with (two or three at the most), and ignore the rest.

Don't

1
Give them too many creative solutions/ options otherwise you'll be asked to sit in 130 whiteboard meetings to discuss each one in depth for the next five years. Better to say you have no solutions and ask them for theirs.

2
Give them your real email address.

3
Get attached to the cause. Remember... before THEY came to YOU, you'd never even heard of famine!

Expert information by
Martin Hughes, WEFAIL

Mail Order Chickens

Agency
WEFAIL

Designed/Developed by
Jordan Stone and
Martin Hughes

Software
Flash, Photoshop

Awards
FWA Site Of The Day,
Cannes Cyber Lion

Launched
2005

www.wefail.com/cockaid

I spy with my little eye

Agency
Achtung!

Designed by
Emile Dekker

Developed by
Willem Hein Triemstra

Software
Flash, Photoshop, Maya,
After Effects

Awards
FWA Site Of The Day

Launched
2006

www.kinderenindekou.nl

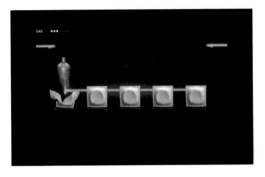

Hope Garden

Agency
Richter7 and Paul Mayne

Designed/Developed by
Paul Mayne

Software
Flash, Fireworks, Photoshop

Awards
FWA Site Of The Day,
Flash Forward Finalist,
Adobe Site Of The Day

Launched
2006

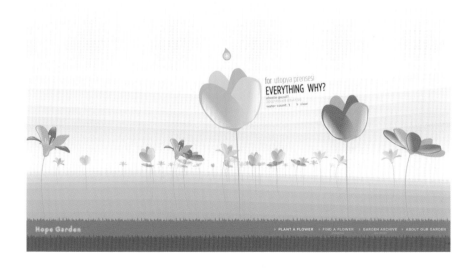

Although it's more easily comprehended as "concept," attitude is something that digs a little deeper into the emotional level. It is often delivered in a simple statement, mood, theme, or combination of all these elements but to most of us the easier association would be through a character.

Attitude when portrayed through the medium of creative design is a clear statement of an idea and a very powerful tool that "hooks" the target audience for often, a very long time. Just a reminder… misuse of it on the other hand may create negative perception amongst the audience that consequently "boxes" the creator into a deep hole.

Do	Don't
1 Open your eyes and mind to your immediate environment. There is creativity everywhere.	1 Become an extremist. Life is hardly black and white. Experiment with many styles and ideas.
2 Try and understand as much as you can about the concept of time and space before you decide to morph it into an attitude.	2 Hide your thoughts too deeply, which can make it hard for the viewer to understand your goal.
3 Listen to your peers, seniors and subordinates as much as you can, do as much research as possible in understanding characters, personality and traits but when the time comes, be decisive.	3 Be afraid to go back to the drawing board if you feel your output has deviated away from your original concepts.

Expert information by
Johnny Choi, Neostream

Eminem

Agency
WEFAIL

Designed by
Jordan Stone and
Martin Hughes

Developed by
Martin Hughes and
Jordan Stone

Software
Photoshop, Flash

Awards
FWA People's Choice
Award, FWA Site Of The
Month, SXSW

Launched
2005

www.wefail.com/eminem

Have Attitude

Hungry Suitcase

Agency
Big Spaceship/Arnold

Designed/Developed by
Big Spaceship/Arnold

Software
Flash

Awards
FWA Site Of The Day

Launched
2007

http://archive.bigspaceship.
com/hungrysuitcase

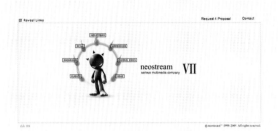

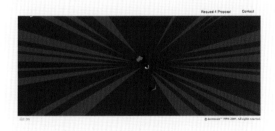

Agency
Neostream

Designed by
Kody Lee

Developed by
Martin Cho

Software
Flash, 3ds Max, Illustrator, Photoshop

Awards
FWA People's Choice Award, FWA Site Of The Day, Ultrashock Bombshock

Launched
2002

www.neostream.com

02 Marketing & Communication

The interactive quality of the web is one of the main features that sets it apart from other mediums. Interaction means allowing users to actively engage with the world you have created on your site, with the text, graphics, sound and animations. It can be everything from simple feedback when they move their mouse over a link, to complex interactive story structures.

It is important to find the appropriate level of interaction for the site at hand. Adding complex interaction might only distract from what you want to say, and create a jittery user experience. On the other hand, when you do manage to find the right level of interaction, it can give your users a deeper understanding and connection with your site.

Do

1
Put together logical information/story units of your content and make a flowchart.

2
Try shifting the structure around and see what happens to the user experience.

3
Create interactive elements that are in tune with the overall design and feel of the site.

Don't

1
Create interaction just for the sake of it.

2
Complicate things; try testing the site on your mom or your boss, to check how less computer-literate people perceive it.

3
Care too much about these rules for interaction. In order to create something interesting you might need to do the unexpected.

Expert information by
Petter Westlund, B-Reel

In-synch Challenge

Agency
Fallon and B-Reel

Designed by
Eric Frost

Developed by
Niklas Lindström

Software
Flash

Awards
FWA Site Of The Month,
Most Influential Flash
Website of 2006

Launched
2006

www.travelersinsynch.com/
challenge_popup.html

Adobe – The Creative Mind

Agency
Goodby, Silverstein &
Partners and unit9

Designed by
Keith Anderson, Mark Sikes,
Spencer Riviera, Kenna
Takahashi, Mike Barbeau

Developed by
Unit 9, Mike Geiger

Software
Flash, Photoshop, Illustrator

Awards
FWA Site Of The Month

Launched
2006

http://www.unit9.com/
creativemind/

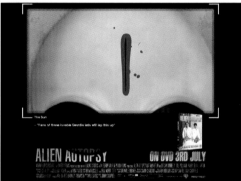

Alien Autopsy

Agency
Franki&Jonny

Designed by
Franki Goodwin

Developed by
Jonny Green

Software
Flash, Photoshop, TextMate,
Ruby-on-Rails

Awards
FWA Site Of The Day

Launched
2006

http://alienautopsy.
frankiandjonny.com

It's that simple, and that hard. Creating a moment (or a dozen moments) that bring true joy and humour to someone's day is usuall a bit more complicated than simply uploading a goofy video. In fact, oftentimes, it's the simple idea, served up in a way no one has seen before. It's the view of our world from an unusual or twisted angle.

Do

1
Make it easy. Smiling shouldn't be work.

2
Be unique. Most things are only funny once.

3
Build in multiple layers of humour and let your visitors discover them.

Don't

1
Laugh at your own jokes.

2
Think it will get funnier with time. It won't.

3
Think local. (The best ideas and humour are universal.)

Expert information by
T. Scott Major & Michael Hart, mono

Make People Smile

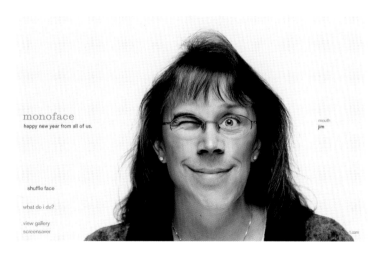

monoface

Agency
mono

Designed by
mono

Developed by
Jim Park

Software
Photoshop, Flash

Awards
FWA Site Of The Day

Launched
2007

http://mono-1.com/
monoface

Email has fast become the most popular form of communication in the digital age and as such can provide a potent channel for developing a dialogue with your audience. A well designed newsletter, sent to a willing list at predetermined, regular intervals can provide a powerful addition to any company's or individual's marketing activity.

If successful, the benefits of producing a newsletter are obvious – as the communication is "pushed" to the end user, you do not need to rely on your audience visiting a website to provide them with the latest information.

Whether you are providing goods, services or news content, get it right and you will have opened a powerful new channel of direct communication with your target audience.

Do

1
Instil confidence in your target audience. Terms and Conditions should be available to your potential subscribers and simple *unsubscribe* options visible at all times.

2
Test your newsletter! Send the final email to numerous email accounts (including web based mail clients such as Gmail and Hotmail) to highlight any potential problems.

3
Keep it clear and concise.

Don't

1
Use plug-ins or JavaScript in HTML newsletters. They will not work.

2
Use the Cc field when sending your newsletter to subscribers. There's no greater faux pas than exposing all your readers email addresses to each other!

3
Forget the *Unsubscribe* link in your email. Whilst you don't want to encourage people to unsubscribe, you MUST offer readers the option.

Expert information by
Rick Palmer, BLOC

Samsung Life Style
Newsletter

Agency
Soleil Noir

Designed/Developed by
Soleil Noir

Software
Photoshop

Launched
2007

FWA Newsletter

Agency
Bloc Media

Designed by
John Denton

Developed by
Xavier Monvoisin

Software
Photoshop, BBEdit

Launched
2006

www.thefwa.com/
members/news0107.html

Agency
WA007

Designed/Developed by
James Begera

Software
Flash, ASP, Photoshop,
Dreamweaver

Launched
2007

www.wa007.com/
newswire/jan2007

Personality — I guess it is something that we all have. However some people's personalities are not something that we would want to see on the Internet. But like me, some people really don't care and put their stuff up anyway. This is when you will discover, by putting yourself out there, some people will love you for it and of course, a lot of people will hate you for it. There's really no middle ground, but I guess that is why using personality on the web has such a strong impact.

Do

1
Realize that not everyone is going to like you. Sometimes people may even hate you.

Don't

2
Work with cool people, because you don't want other people's lame personalities rubbing off on you.

1
Take it personally when people don't like your personality.

2
Worry about offending someone.

3
Make up a good personality if you don't have one, remember people lie about themselves on the Internet all of the time.

3
Lie about yourself. Too many people lie about themselves on the Internet.

Expert information by
James Dvorak, LitFuse

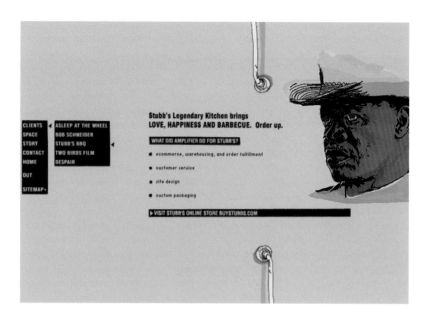

Amplifier

Agency
sofake

Designed/Developed by
Jordan Stone

Software
Photoshop, Flash

Awards
FWA Site Of The Month,
SXSW

Launched
2004

www.archive.amplifier.
sofake.com

LitFuse Design

Agency
LitFuse

Designed by
James Dvorak,
Scott Ichikawa

Developed by
James Dvorak

Software
Photoshop, Illustrator, Flash

Awards
FWA Site Of The Month

Launched
2006

Freedom Interactive Design

Agency
Freedom Interactive

Designed/Developed by
Freedom Interactive

Software
Flash

Awards
FWA Site Of The Day,
Flash Forward Nominee

Launched
2004

http://demos.
freedomandpartners.com/
fid/main.htm

As a strategic digital agency, showcasing your design work and creative executions in an engaging and concise manner is absolutely paramount. It's important to recognise that the first impression prospective clients will potentially have of your agency will be conveyed via your portfolio. As with all first impressions, you should ensure that you put your best foot forward.

Do

1
Ensure that your creative portfolio is scalable and flexible enough to showcase your most recent work as expeditiously as possible.

2
Come up with a consistent methodology to present your work in an engaging fashion.

3
Plan your portfolio as if its sole objective is to tell a story. Be sure to highlight the key components and attributes in a succinct and meaningful manner.

Don't

1
Make it overly cumbersome or complicated, where it would require months of production to showcase your work.

2
Show emotional content in a static or copy centric presentation. For example, still imagery and screenshots would most likely not be adequate to convey the sensory experience of an advergame or viral video.

3
Lock yourself into a design that doesn't lend itself to scalability, thus hindering the ability to have your portfolio grow with you.

Expert information by
Richard Lent, AgencyNet

North Kingdom

Agency
North Kingdom

Designed by
Robert Lindström

Developed by
Klas Kroon

Software
Flash, Photoshop

Awards
FWA Site Of The Day

Launched
2005

AgencyNet Interactive

Agency
Agencynet

Designed/Developed by
Agencynet team

Software
Flash, After Effects,
Photoshop, Lightwave 3D

Awards
FWA Site Of the Month, FWA
Site Of The Day, Ultrashock
Bombshock, Cannes Cyber
Lion Shortlist, WMA Best
Interactive Services Website

Launched
2005

www.agencynet.com

Fantasy Interactive

Agency
Fantasy Interactive
(Swedish Office)

Designed by
David Hugh Martin

Developed by
Rickard Leckstrom

Software
Photoshop, Flash, Maya

Awards
FWA Site Of the Month, FWA
Site Of The Day, Ultrashock
Bombshock

Launched
2004

www.f-i.com

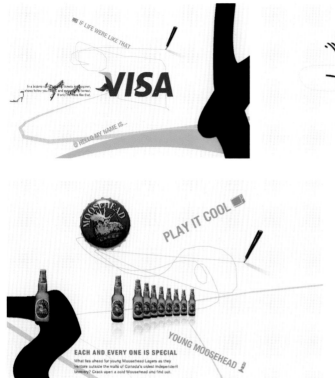

Leoburnett.ca

Agency
Arc Worldwide, Toronto
– a Leo Burnett Company

Designed by
Peter Gomes

Developed by
Dan Purdy

Software
Flash

Awards
FWA Site Of The Year,
Golden Drum, Arc
Worldwide Practical
Magic, ANDY, Webby, Clio,
D&AD, One Show, Cannes
Cyber Lion, ADC Toronto,
Campaign Digital, New York
Festivals, Communication
Arts, Flash Forward, Adobe
& FWA Site of The Decade
nominee, LIAA, CMA, Young
Guns, Mobius, Applied Arts

Launched
2005

www.leoburnett.ca

Most careers limit self-promotion to *curricula vitae* buried in job search engines. A personal interactive portfolio is an unparalleled creative opportunity to introduce yourself and your work to the world.

Do

1
Bring your projects to life with some form of storytelling.

2
Show a diversity of work that emphasises conceptual thinking.

3
Be yourself.

Don't

1
Distract or somehow take the focus away from your work.

2
Make any loading and transition animations overly long and superfluous.

3
Have an ego.

Expert information by
Dave Werner, Minor Studios

Agency
Dave Werner

Designed/Developed by
Dave Werner

Software
Photoshop, After Effects,
Flash, iMovie

Awards
FWA Site Of the Month,
FWA Site Of The Day, 85th
Annual Art Director's Club
Interactive Distinctive Merit

Launched
2006

http://okaydave.com

Noe Design

Agency
Dan Noe

Designed/Developed by
Dan Noe

Software
Flash, After Effects

Awards
FWA Site Of The Day,
Communication Arts, FITC,
ADAI, Gold Addy Award, ITA

Launched
2004

www.noedesign.com/2005/
index.html

Agency
Greg Washington

Designed/Developed by
Greg Washington

Software
Illustrator, Photoshop, Flash

Awards
FWA Site of The Day, Flash
Forward Silver, May 1st
Reboot Winner

Launched
2004

Totality of actions, sometimes very creative ones, can be pursued to achieve better search engine rankings.

It's interesting to see how code optimisation improvements are moving towards the fact that there is a broad use of Flash as a primary technology in many important projects. The main challenge will be to have a full Flash site outshining a regular HTML-oriented site in terms of indexation.

Can Flash win today? Is it pure fantasy? No. There will always be a difference between a popular site due to hi-tech indexation and a popular one due to exciting contents. The second one will always be on top!

Do

1
Create a full Flash-oriented website only if your intentions are to make it unique.

2
Invent! Ideas are always at the base of success.

3
Use the external API interface if you want to simulate HTML navigation without losing the interactive strength of a Flash project.

Don't

1
Think Flash isn't capable of high indexing as an HTML solution.

2
Think that only the most popular SEO solutions are right.

3
Concentrate on a one-software platform solution. Unity is strength.

Expert information by
Fabio De Gregorio, Drink Creativity!

Alari Park Group

Agency
Drink Creativity!

Designed by
Fabio De Gregorio

Developed by
Fabio De Gregorio,
Romina Mattina, Luca Milan

Software
Flash, Photoshop, ASP.NET,
SQL, JS, XML

Awards
FWA Site Of The Day

Launched
2007

DAKINE

Agency
2Advanced Studios

Designed by
2Advanced Studios,
DAKINE

Developed by
Mike Matz, Sean Berry, Ryan
Serra (2Advanced Studios)

Software
Flash, Photoshop,
Dreamweaver

Launched
2007

www.dakine.com

James Martin – Chef

Agency
Webshocker

Designed by
Matjaz Valentar

Developed by
Matjaz Valentar, Grega Carni

Software
Flash, Photoshop,
After Effects

Awards
FWA Site Of The Day

Launched
2007

www.jamesmartinchef.co.uk

Think Swedish

Agency
Fantasy Interactive

Designed/Developed by
Fantasy Interactive

Software
Flash, Photoshop, .NET Web
Services

Awards
FWA Site Of The Day

Launched
2007

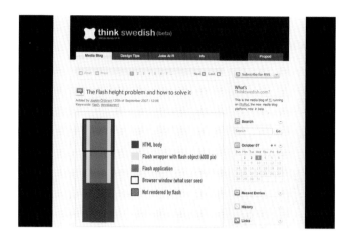

If you could restart your life from anywhere or at any time you like, how much value would you see in the moment right now? And, how much excitement would you see in a reversible life?

In movies and novels, a story is often linear and in a sense it's meant to be conveyed to others almost always in this fashion. Plus, the reality and excitement of a story might only be possible by its linear and compulsive nature.

However, interactive-storytelling is not held by any rules or regulations, it can be what it wants to be. With this in mind, the possibilities are endless.

If you were to provide multiple paths (in a story), it may mean that these paths all need to be impressive both in quality and quantity. So, it is worth considering that although telling a story may create its own challenges, you may be in for more success if you actually go beyond the conventional parameters and allow the story to evolve freely.

Do

1
Experience various kinds of stories as much as possible.

2
Keep thinking: What is a story?

3
Entertain your audience by any means.

Don't

1
Create points of hesitation; keep the story moving along smoothly.

2
Be stereotyped in your approach. Originality always wins the day.

3
Expect your audience to behave as you might expect.

Expert information by
Yutaka Kodama, Bascule Inc.

Tell a Story

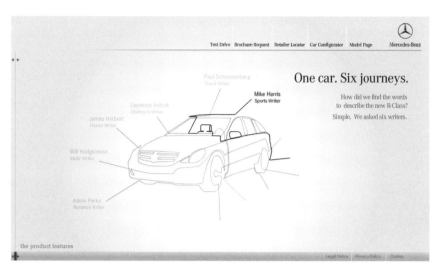

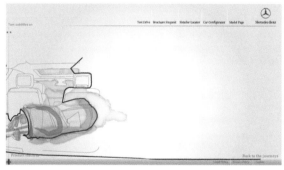

Mercedes-Benz R-Class,
Six Journeys

Agency
Agency Republic

Designed by
Jim Stump, Ben Harris,
Gemma Butler, Gavin
Gordon-Rogers

Developed by
Richard Lainchbury, Odin
Church, Adam Robertson

Software
Flash, After Effects

Awards
FWA Site Of The Day,
IAB Creative Showcase

Launched
2006

www.mercedes-benz.
co.uk/sixjourneys

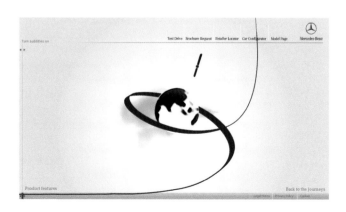

Tell a Story

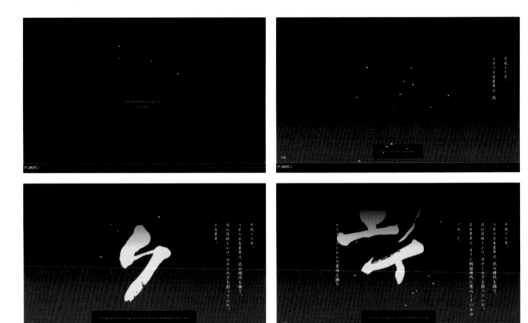

The Creative Bushido

Agency
Bascule Inc.

Designed by
Shin Takeuchi, Mayo Tobita

Developed by
Shigeo Sugiyama

Software
Flash

Awards
FWA Site Of The Month,
4th Tokyo Interactive Ad
Awards Website Corporate
Site Bronze

Launched
2006

www.yomiko.co.jp/bushido

I'm a Cyborg, but that's okay

Agency
d.o.E.S

Designed by
Hyunah Yoon

Developed by
Sang June Lee

Software
Flash, 3ds Max, Photoshop

Awards
FWA Site Of The Day

Launched
2006

www.d-o-e-s.com/
collection/cyborg

A successful viral campaign is defined by how many people within your target have shared it. To make a great one, you first need to understand what drives people to share experiences.

At the very root, people share experiences as a way to socialize and form meaningful relationships with each other. They share experiences, objects and ideas that inspire conversation, build community, encourage laughter, and allow them to express their personality. They're particularly interested in sharing things that communicate their positive image.

If brand experiences allow for personal expression and make consumers appear hip, funny, caring, or smart, they are likely to be shared. Creating branded content that will be shared by consumers is not just an exercise in marketing; it's a sociological study and an engagement with anthropology and pop culture.

Do

1
Be relevant and in all the right places.

2
Keep it simple and focused (experiences have to be easy to share).

3
Allow the consumer to mess with your brand.

Don't

1
Create an experience with barriers of entry such as registration (unless you have a great hook).

2
Expect the consumer to wait too long for the payoff.

3
Reinvent the wheel. Use the tools out there that are already proven to craft and deliver your experiences.

Expert information by
Winston Binch & Wojtek Szumowski, Crispin, Porter + Bogusky

The Whopperettes

Agency
Crispin, Porter + Bogusky

Designed
Alex Bogusky, Andrew
Keller, Rob Reilly, Jeff
Benjamin, John Parker,
Mark Taylor, Evan Fry, Bob
Cianfrone, Chean Wei Law,
Thomas Rodgers

Developed by
EVB

Software
Flash

Awards
FWA Site Of The Day,
Cannes Gold, LIAA Finalist,
Shots Grand Prix

Launched
2006

http://wwwawards.
cpbgroup.com/awards/
whopperettesoneshow.html

Here's the main gate, the invitation, the beginning… your homepage.
There's someone knocking at your door on the web and you've got a split second to catch their attention, show them who you are and invite them to explore. The task is much harder than hosting a guest at your own house… you don't know who's coming, when or what their reaction will be and what the dress code is. But you still want to make them feel good.
The homepage is probably one of the hardest things to put out there, also being one of the most important parts of a company's or individual's image. If first impressions are still crucial in the digital age, the homepage has to be your most delicate and powerful tool.

Do

1
Show the real you. Try to make the homepage reflect your character, attitude and qualities (as an individual or a company).

2
Be creative and have fun. It's the Internet — go crazy. People will appreciate it.

3
Allow them to contact you easily. A website is a great form of communication, but nothing beats a direct email exchange or a chat on the phone. Make that contact info inviting and visible at all times.

Don't

1
Be too modest. Someone's here to find out about you, so fire away and show them your best.

2
Make them wait. It's not the movies. People won't wait to see the main feature, so cut down on the number of clicks and the loading times.

3
Try to blend in. There's nothing worse than trying to look "as good" as your competition. You are different, so make it show.

Expert information by
Bartek Gołębiowski, Click5

guraphic designer 3N
(My Face)

Agency
Sun-Han Kwon

Designed/Developed by
Sun-Han Kwon

Software
Photoshop, Flash

Awards
FWA Site Of The Day,
7th Blue League Silver

Launched
2006

www.guraphic.com/
guraphic

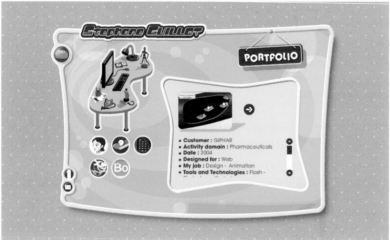

Stephane Guillot

Agency
Stephane Guillot

Designed/Developed by
Stephane Guillot

Software
Flash, Photoshop, Illustrator,
SoundForge, Dreamweaver,
Acid

Awards
FWA Site of the Day,
Ultrashock Bombshock,
ITA Site Of The Week

Launched
2005

www.stephaneguillot.com/
index_uk.htm

ManaMediaGroup

Agency
Click5

Designed by
Adam Nieszporek, Tomasz
Wozniak

Developed by
Adam Nieszporek

Software
Flash, 3ds Max, After Effects

Awards
FWA Site Of The Day

Launched
2006

www.manamediagroup.com

Technology & Programming

Introduction by
<u>Eric Jordan</u>, 2Advanced Studios

03

As a web designer who has been building sites for nearly 11 years now, to say that the way I approach creating websites today versus in the past has "changed slightly" would be such a gross understatement that it would probably merit committing me to a psychiatric institution. I have gone from creating simple brochureware pages to managing entire campaigns that centre on using new technologies to improve the effectiveness of websites and even web applications. Myself aside, I'm willing to bet that just about every website developer will tell you that they do things very differently these days. Although the Internet is still young, we all know that it is one of the fastest growing mediums in all of history. Its growth continues to accelerate at an amazing pace, and at the same time, the race to be on the bleeding-edge of web technology intensifies.

"We make it our mission to stay keenly aware of nearly every technological development that arises in the web world."

As I write this there is a group of people sitting in a dimly lit room somewhere, surrounded by the glow of computers, and they are brainstorming about how they can use the latest technological advancements to get ahead of the competition on the web. Someone might be suggesting the use of advanced metrics to track user movement through the site; another person might be pushing the use of Flash Media Server for its live video capabilities, and yet another person might be urging the development of a rich media application that allows for product personalisation and customisation.

Quite frankly, websites are not just websites anymore. Having a URL on the Internet means a lot more today than it did a few years ago. Today, websites are huge marketing mechanisms that only seem relevant if they are robust and offer a cutting edge experience that is a step above the rest. It's not terribly difficult to see that things have evolved since the days of GIF slices and the birth of Flash. Megabytes have become terabytes, hit counters have become metrics tracking, and anything that isn't static has become a rich media experience with fullscreen interactive video, 3D visualisation and 192 bit streaming audio. All in all, it's pretty clear that we are in a whole new ball game.

Are we clear?
Crystal.

Okay, now that we are all in agreement that the web world is significantly different than it was just a few years ago, just what about its technology has changed? How can programming aid in improving a website? And more importantly, how can it be achieved? It doesn't do any good to fool yourself, or your client, into thinking that great animation and impressive graphics will cut it alone. Today, clients are very savvy and want to see real, tangible results from their website. They want to be able to measure the effectiveness of their site, and desire real-world feedback as to what is working and what is not working. Additionally, and perhaps the most interesting and paradoxical aspect of modern web development, they want their website to have a certain human quality. We are so suffocated by automated systems and mechanized responses these days that many companies seek new ways of communicating and connecting with people on a human level. Surprisingly, this is where technology and programming can actually shine.

"We are so suffocated by automated systems and mechanized responses these days that many companies seek new ways of communicating and connecting with people on a human level."

Any technology or programmatic element that can be brought to bear on a website's ability to perform a specific function makes it smarter and therefore more effective. This is the reason that my design studio has a division dedicated solely to website programming, because our clients seek these types of enhancements. We make it our mission to stay keenly aware of nearly every technological development that arises in the web world. As a company focused on developing advanced websites for the modern world, we are responsible for understanding our client's ultimate goal and how to achieve that goal. Quite simply, it is our job to understand cutting edge web technology and how it can improve the end product that we develop for a client.

Today, it is rare for us to be working on a project that doesn't involve some sort of development effort, be it implementing a custom CMS (Content Management System) in order to enable the client to manage the dynamic aspects of their site, or integrating some form of web analytics platform such as Fireclick or Omniture. We have also been involved in architecting and building sophisticated web applications, ranging from audio mixing interfaces to product customisation modules, to 3D avatar designers. All were custom engineered from the ground up by our development team, which is made up of very talented individuals who have a passion for learning new technologies. This passion has kept our clients coming back to us, because we are willing to approach websites in new and different ways, using technology and programming to make sites more intelligent.

I believe the key lies in adaptation, to have the ability to embrace new technology and evolve with it. If you keep yourself open to learning new technologies and find enjoyment in challenging yourself with learning the new advancements that come along, you will allow yourself the ability to flex and adapt to changes in the industry. This is the best way to stay ahead of the game in the business of building websites, because you will always be able to provide the most cutting-edge services to your client. However, there is no rulebook for this sort of thing. Every day presents us with a new challenge, a new problem to solve, most often something that has never been attempted before. Our passion for overcoming technological barriers is what helps us succeed in these situations. We believe that we have something to contribute to the advancement of technology as a whole, and so should you. Together, we are all shaping the landscape of the web. These are uncharted waters for most of us, and for that reason it is important to continue learning and evolving. Technological advancement is a collective effort, a cooperative process of invention and innovation, and we all have a part to play.

"Every day presents us with a new challenge, a new problem to solve, most often something that has never been attempted before. Our passion for overcoming technological barriers is what helps us succeed in these situations."

Eric Jordan
2Advanced Studios

Bio.
Eric Jordan
2Advanced Studios

Eric Jordan, the creative visionary behind 2Advanced Studios, leverages his extensive background in motion graphics and cutting edge new media technologies to create high impact solutions for our clientele. Over the past seven years, Eric has led the 2Advanced team to the forefront of the design industry. Having delivered on over 680 studio projects, Eric's creative direction and inspiration drive home the company vision for "Progressive Design Technology."

Today, Eric is as "hands on" as ever and continues to receive wide industry acclaim for his mastery of a wide array of tools, including Flash, Cinema 4D, After Effects, Photoshop, Illustrator, Combustion, and a host of other products. He has contributed to countless book and magazine publications, and has received numerous industry awards and recognition. Notably, Eric is credited with starting a progressive design movement that has influenced design culture around the globe and has led 2Advanced Studios to be recognised as one of the most cutting edge design firms in the industry.
–
www.2advanced.com

"Websites are not just websites anymore."

When we think broadband, it's all about taking advantage of the Internet's big pipes and faster downloads. In terms of a website, it allows us to create bigger and more complex Flash experiences.

Using full-page integrated videos becomes a much more viable option than before. For us, doing movie and entertainment websites means we can utilise motion graphics video techniques instead of relying on old school Flash animation techniques. For us, broadband means actualising and sharing the exact visual idea we want to convey. Broadband means brand new experiences in website design. Broadband means embracing and massaging new technology.

Do

1
Think outside the box. This sounds oh so cliché but it's really the biggest hurdle to overcome. Don't just rehash the same techniques and animation tricks.

2
Understand the newest technologies. Keeping on top of these developments really helps in creating the most impactful broadband websites.

3
Test! Test! Test! Nothing is really done until it's tested online in as many variations as possible.

Don't

1
Stop pushing the boundaries. In web design, it's easy to become stagnant and accept that what everyone else is doing is what we're limited to.

2
Spend all your time in R&D. Before starting your project, you should already understand the possibilities as well as the limitations.

3
Underestimate the impact of small details. An abundance of small details makes up for big impact.

Expert information by
Jeff Lin, Hybrid Studio, Inc.

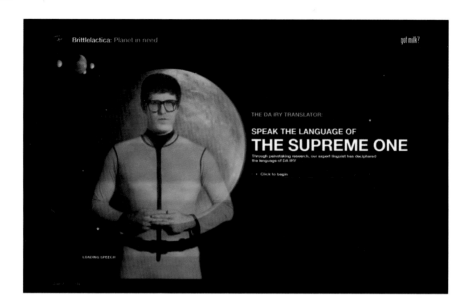

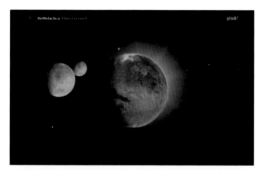

Planet In Need

Agency
Goodby, Silverstein
& Partners and North
Kingdom

Designed by
Jeff Goodby, Will
McGinness, Robert
Lindström, Feh Tarty, Ronny
Northrop, Pat McKay, Paul
Charney, Mike Geiger

Developed by
Mike Geiger, David Eriksson,
Roger Stighall, Charlotta
Lundqvist, Kenny Lindström,
Mikael Forsgren, Klas
Kroon, Tomas Westermark,
Daniel Wallstrom, Mathias
Lindgren, Martha Jurzynski,
Debbie Lee

Software
Flash, Photoshop, Final Cut,
Illustrator

Awards
FWA Site Of The Day,
Cannes Cyber Lion Gold x2,
LIAA Gold x2

Launched
2006

http://demo.northkingdom.
com/gotmilk/planetinneed

Nowadays the vast majority of websites are database driven. They are template-based systems displaying dynamic data, where programming on one hand and content production on the other are two strictly separated processes. For this purpose they are provided with a content management system (the 3 letter word is CMS), which is basically a non-technical platform that should allow them to populate a database without any (or with very little) technical knowledge.

There's very complex software around that often needs extensive tailoring as opposed to some very simple systems.

Do

1
Make sure that you're not reinventing the wheel. Only begin creating your own CMS if you really can't find what you need already available.

2
Make your CMS as generic as possible. Use building blocks that can be reused and separately tailored according to specific needs.

3
Keep in mind that usability should be your main concern: each title, input field, label name, help text, etc.

You'll achieve the ultimate usability goal if your audience can start using your CMS without explanations and without a manual.

Don't

1
Build the 133.467th version of PHP-MyAdmin.

2
Make your CMS more complex than necessary.

3
Offer options that cannot be used sensibly.

Expert information by
Pascal Leroy, group94

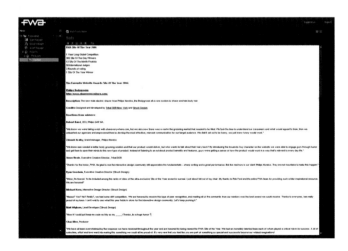

theFWA.com CMS

Designed by
Graham Stinson, Nathan Young

Developed by
Jason Hickner, Jared Wray, Brannon Jones

Software
Flash

Launched
2005

www.thefwa.com/
taschen2007/fwacms.html

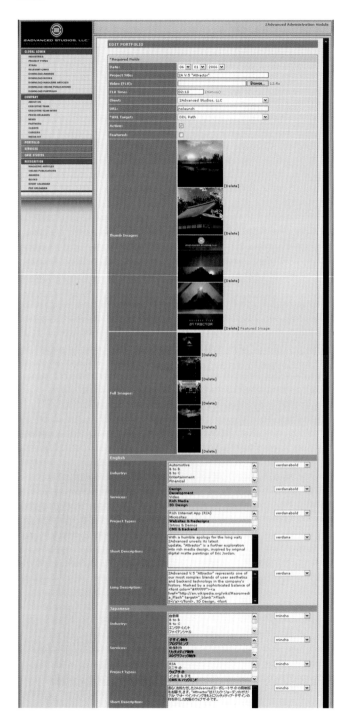

2Advanced Studios CMS

Agency
2Advanced Studios

Designed by
Eric Jordan

Developed by
Sonny Kotler, Ryan Serra

Launched
2006

http://www.thefwa.
com/taschen2007/
2advancedcms.html

group94's flash94 CMS

Agency
group94

Designed/Developed by
group94

Software
Flash, PHP, MySQL

Launched
2006

www.thefwa.com/
taschen2007/g94cms.html

03 Technology & Programming

141

The Internet is essentially an electronic library of books written by billions of authors. Paper books are static: once they are printed they do not change, but the pages of an electronic book can change at any time... they are dynamic.

Being dynamic means the content of the page, the very words and images that form the document, can be altered as you read it, or altered depending on how you or other people use it.

This opens up a whole world of opportunities, but at the same time opens up a can of design worms. Knowing where and when to use dynamic content is an art in itself.

Do

1
Think of the user. Always consider your website or application from your user's point of view, not your own prejudices.

2
Keep it intuitive. Dynamic content can help you keep instructions to a minimum: less need for page reloads, extra arrows or links.

3
Take inspiration from other dynamic sites. Only by seeing what works and what doesn't can you understand what being dynamic really means.

Don't

1
Use technology just because you can. Use dynamic content only when it improves the experience, not just because a certain acronym or whizz-bang gadget is all the rage.

2
Believe your own hype. Ask yourself, would you use it? If not, ask yourself why not and re-evaluate your design.

3
Be afraid to change your design. Because it's dynamic it can always be revised at a later date.

Expert information by
Paul Neave, Neave

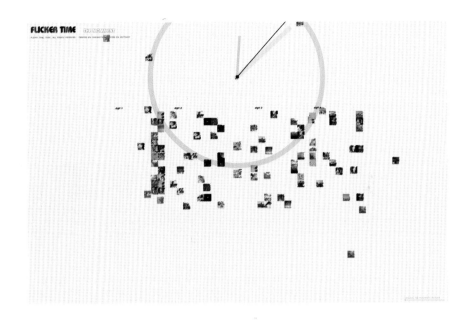

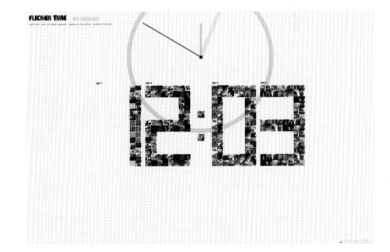

Flickr Time

Agency
Hiroshi Tazawa

Designed/Developed by
Hiroshi Tazawa

Software
Flash

Awards
FWA Site Of The Day

Launched
2006

www.hottoast.org/
convexstyle/flickrtime

amaztype

Agency
tha ltd.

Designed/Developed by
Yugo Nakamura

Software
Flash

Awards
FWA Site Of The Day

Launched
2005

www.amaztype.tha.jp

Flash Earth

Agency
Paul Neave

Designed/Developed by
Paul Neave

Software
Flash

Awards
FWA Site Of The Day

Launched
2005

www.flashearth.com

145

For all its vast breadth the Internet is still a relatively new technology, and one still finding its forms. However, all too often the commercial need for the familiar and non-threatening results in this new medium, a medium capable of marvellous fluidity, resembling the printed page.

Enter the "experimental" sites. Usually relegated to entertainment and personal projects, it's in these sites that new forms and new systems of information display are emerging. If they do their job well these new forms may themselves become the "familiar and non-threatening" and shape the future face of the Internet.

They are also an opportunity to have some serious fun. In the case of personal projects, free from commercial restraints, you can finally let your imagination run riot.

Do	**Don't**
1 Follow up unexpected results. Strange things can occur when you experiment and following a tangential path may lead to an interesting place.	**1** Be afraid of failure. It's only by experimenting that you'll find out if that idea is a good one. And whatever the result, no one's going to die.
2 Look beyond the web for ideas and metaphors. Mankind has been organizing things for thousands of years, nature for millions.	**2** Hesitate to rip it up and start again if it's really not working.
3 Pay attention to what your peers are doing. New and exciting techniques can become clichés with ever increasing rapidity.	**3** Pay too much attention to lists such as this. Go break some rules instead!

Expert information by
Andy Foulds, Freelancer Flash Designer/Developer

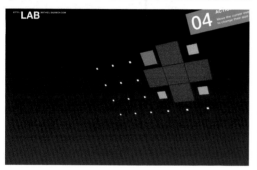

LAB

Agency
Mathieu Badimon

Designed/Developed by
Mathieu Badimon

Software
Flash

Awards
FWA Site Of The Day

Launched
2007

http://lab.mathieu-badimon.
com

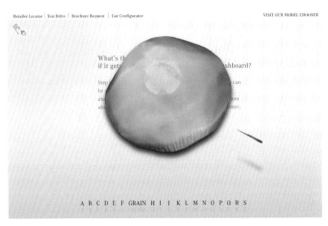

Mercedes a-to-s

Agency
Agency Republic

Designed by
Andy Sandoz, Gavin
Gordon-Rogers, Gemma
Butler, Marga Arrom-Bibiloni

Developed by
Robin Wong, Richard
Lainchbury, Andy Foulds

Software
Flash, Photoshop, Illustrator,
PHP

Awards
FWA Site Of The Day, One
Show Bronze Pencil, IAB
Creative Showcase. Cannes
Cyber Lions Silver Award,
Campaign Digital Awards,
BIMA

Launched
2006

www.a-to-s.co.uk

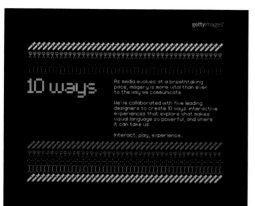

10 ways

Agency
Getty Images and
Great Works

Designed by
Mark Fraser and
Chris Ashworth

Developed by
Less Rain, Tomato,
and Sumona

Software
ASP, Flash, PHP, MySQL

Awards
FWA Site Of The Day, How
Interactive Design Award,
Gold EurobestLive 2006
Interactive

Launched
2006

By adding Flash components to HTML structures, hybrid sites utilise the best features that the two technologies have to offer. While HTML provides a means to organize searchable text and imagery, Flash enables the integration of motion, video, sound, robust applications and microsites to truly enhance the user experience.

Hybrid sites provide the client maximum exposure for their content, while delivering the maximum impact to the target audience. In other words, hybrid sites are the solution to make otherwise boring sites into exciting, encompassing online experiences.

Do

1
Use Flash detection to replace important interactive items like navigation with HTML versions if the person does not have the correct version of Flash installed.

2
Keep any important links (and text) outside of Flash so that search engines can easily traverse the entire site.

3
Use the external interface API if you want to mimic full Flash site interactivity by talking to multiple Flash movies on a page. Give feedback, not only for your visitors, but also for yourself.

Don't

1
Use frames unless you plan on taking the time to integrate deep linking capabilities and make all textual content accessible to search engines.

2
Make your Flash navigation file size so large that it takes too long to download.

3
Have annoying Flash animation build-ins on things like navigation that re-animate on every page of the site.

Expert information by
Shane Seminole Mielke, 2Advanced Studios

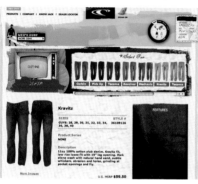

O'Neill

Agency
2Advanced Studios

Designed by
Shane Mielke

Developed by
Kevan Norr, Sonny Kotler

Software
Flash, After Effects,
Photoshop

Awards
FWA Site Of The Day, Step
Inside Design's Best of
Web, Horizon Interactive
Awards Silver, Summit
Creative Awards Bronze,
HOW Interactive Awards
Outstanding Design,
Marcom Creative Awards
Gold, Macromedia Site Of
The Day, W3 Awards Gold

Launched
2005

Magnum Photos – In Motion

Agency
group94

Designed by
group94

Developed by
group94 and
Enzym Denmark

Software
FreeHand, Flash,
Photoshop, TopStyle,
Final Cut Pro, asp.net

Awards
FWA Site Of The Day

Launched
2006

http://inmotion.
magnumphotos.com

The 4400 season 2

Agency
Firstborn

Designed/Developed by
Firstborn

Software
Flash, XML, CSS, HTML, Javascript

Awards
FWA Site Of The Day

Launched
2005

www.firstbornmultimedia.
com/websites/119_usa_
THE4400_S2

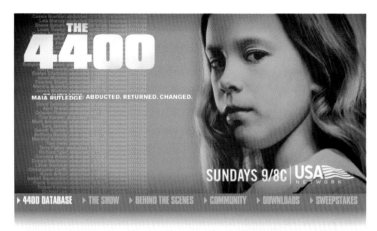

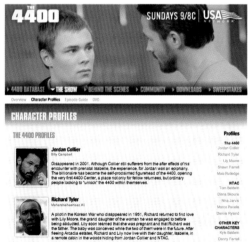

The ability to search through a website, using keywords, phrases, products or codes, is a very useful feature for the end user, especially within large sites with extensive content. Should a search facility be included on a website, it should be placed in a prominent position and should appear in the same position on every page to form continuity.

Searching for specific criteria within a website makes finding relevant information easy. Tagging your own keywords to site content is a real plus too — this enables the webmaster to link related words to website content. For example: The keyword "TV" can be tagged for use in the search for all text picking up the word "television."

Web developers should always consider adding a "Site Search Facility" and such a feature should be a standard part of any CMS (Content Management System).

Do

1
Have the search facility placed in a prominent position and in the same position throughout the site.

2
Categorise search results.

3
Tag your own keywords to the site content.

Don't

1
Make the search facility hard to find.

2
Display too many search results at one time.

3
Make it too complicated for the end user.

Expert information by
Matjaz Valentar, Webshocker

Volkswagen of America

Agency
Crispin, Porter + Bogusky

Designed by/Developed by
Crispin, Porter + Bogusky, Domani Studios, Oshyn, Motive, Hanson Dodge Creative, Squarewave motive, blue rock, 3drecon, iconfactory, Rocket, Driftlab, IQ Interactive, Digital Domain, GTN, Evox, Armstrong & White, With A twist, Spontaneous

Software
Flash, DHTML/Ajax, JBoss, MySQL

Awards
FWA Site Of The Day

Launched
2007

www.vw.com

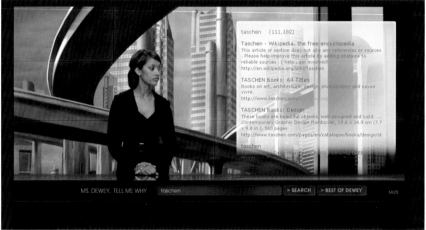

Ms. Dewey

Agency
EVB

Designed by
Microsoft, MRM Partners,
EVB: Jason Zada, Todd Bois

Developed by
EVB: Boris Pique

Software
Flash

Launched
2006

Absolut Search

Agency
Great Works

Designed by
Ted Persson and Sebastien
Vacherot (TBWA\Paris),
Jimmy Poopuu

Developed by
Jocke Wissing, Magnus
Wålsten, Eva Nilsson,
Kristoffer Triumf, Nicolas
Boyer and Alexis Dernov
(TBWA\Paris)

Software
Flash

Awards
FWA Site Of The Day,
EPICA Awards Silver,
Eurobest Bronze

Launched
2006

When was the last time you made an online purchase? Did you add your item(s) to a "shopping cart?" This metaphor is familiar to most Internet users by now, but the basic idea is to save items in order to do something with them later. This concept can be used in many different situations.

School instructors or students could use a "light box" feature to collect images for a class presentation. Once the items have been collected, they could be saved and pulled up again or sent to peers via email. In some cases, websites provide the tools to create a custom slide show presentation complete with titles and annotations.

Imagine an art director at an advertising agency who is searching for the right photographer for their campaign. Photographers could make the art director's job much easier by allowing them to create a customised "portfolio" of work that could be sent to their team or even their client.

Do

1
Remember that if you must make the user log in, make the process as easy as possible.

2
Give users an incentive for logging in.

3
Allow users to remove items after they have been saved.

Don't

1
Assume anything of the user.

2
Forget familiar interface concepts (like "drag-and-drop").

3
Over embellish this feature. It should be simple and easy to use.

Expert information by
JD Hooge, Gridplane

Design Archives

ANNUAL 27   ARCHIVE   SEARCH

THE AIGA DESIGN ARCHIVES ARE A RECORD OF ANNUAL JURIED SELECTIONS OF DESIGN EXCELLENCE and the work of designers honored by AIGA. These interactive archives provide broad accessibility to an extensive collection of contemporary design for research and reference. This definitive resource on American design will continue to expand with each year's new selections and the addition of special collections.

Sponsors | Resources | Membership | Discussions | Terms | Feedback | Credits | ©2007 AIGA

AIGA Design Archives

RETURN   ❮ 21 / 3269 ❯

"Scient's Innovation Acceleration Lab: WorkshopONE"

DESIGN CATEGORY
Experience design, 2001

DESIGN FIRM
Understanding Lab (New York, New York)

COLLECTION
(2002) 365: AIGA Year in Design 23

○ DESCRIPTION ○ CREDITS ○ SHARE 3 COMMENTS

WorkshopONE was a one-day innovation skill-building workshop delivered to more than 2,000 Scient employees and diverse client teams in the firm's Innovation Acceleration Labs located in New York and San Francisco. It was intended to help build an inclusive culture of innovation across the organization.

READ THIS PAGE

MY LIGHTBOX   DRAG IMAGES TO LIGHTBOX

AIGA Design Archives

Agency
Second Story

Designed by
Brad Johnson, Julie Beeler, Jeremy Clark, JD Hooge

Developed by
David Knape, David Brewer, Thomas Wester

Software
Illustrator, Flash, FlashCom, Cold Fusion

Awards
FWA Site Of The Day, Print Interactive Design Annual 2006, SXSW Interactive Web Awards 2006, HOW Interactive Design Annual 2006, Communication Arts Interactive Annual 2005, One Show Interactive Silver Pencil 2005, I.D. Annual Design Review 2005

Launched
2005

http://designarchives.
aiga.org

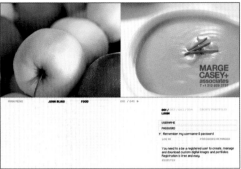

Marge Casey + Associates

Agency
group94

Designed by
group94, Liska NY, Toda NY

Developed by
group94

Software
FreeHand, Illustrator, Flash,
Photoshop, PHP, MySQL

Awards
FWA Site Of The Day

Launched
2004

www.margecasey.com

Sonja Mueller

Agency
Less Rain

Designed by
Matthias Netzberger

Developed by
Oliver Greschke

Software
Flash

Awards
FWA Site Of The Day,
2006 Creative Review
Annual

Launched
2005

www.sonjamueller.org

161

Sites developed with web standards can be accessed by anyone with an Internet enabled device, regardless of disability, hardware or software platform. As an additional bonus, search engines such as Google or Yahoo can do a better job at indexing them, which in turn results in better placement within search results.

In site development, separation of content, presentation and behaviour is of great importance. Once you adopt web standards and principles, and master CSS techniques, development time shortens and your site will be easier to maintain.

Do

1
Create meaning! Structure your content first and consider accessibility aspects. Add all the cool page transitions and animations at the very end — think of it as the final touch for the overall composition.

2
Size text using keywords, ems or percentages to allow text flexibility in older browsers.

3
Test your page on as many browsers/ platforms as possible. Check your site with Flash/JavaScript/ images disabled and provide fallbacks.

Don't

1
Compromise standards for time frame or budget. If they are the limiting factor, consider discussing priorities of other things. Tables for layout are not an option... period.

2
Forget about your users and accessibility.

3
Brag about the site validation. Standards are not about passing the validator, they are about universal access by everyone.

Expert information by
Vanja Bertalan, Burza d.o.o.

Own Your C

Agency
AgencyNet

Designed/Developed by
AgencyNet

Software
Flash, After Effects,
Photoshop, Dreamweaver,
Lightbox JS 2.0, Script.
Aculo.Us

Awards
FWA Site Of The Month,
FWA Site Of The Day,
Stylegala, ITA Site Of The
Week, Communication Arts
Site Of The Week

Launched
2006

www.ownyourc.com/static

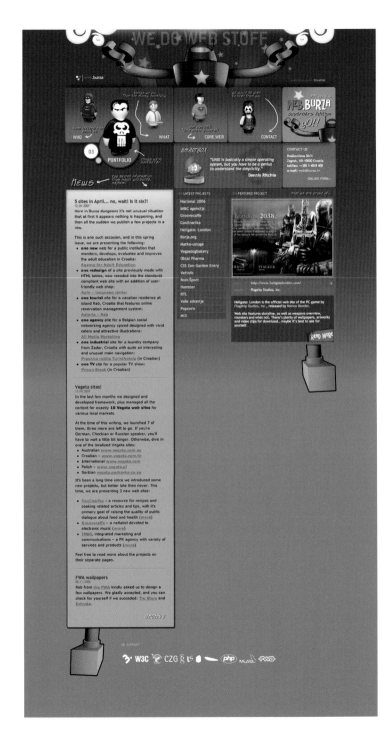

web.burza Superhero
Edition

Agency
Burza d.o.o. (web.burza)

Designed by
Marko Krsul, Slavko Janjic

Developed by
Vanja Bertalan, Marko
Dugonjic, Tomas Trkulja

Software
Photoshop, Flash, PHP,
MySQL

Awards
FWA Site Of The Day, Web
Standards Awards Site Of
The Month, Stylegala All
Stars

Launched
2005

http://web.burza.hr

Brother Jones Artworks

Agency
Keegan Jones

Designed/Developed by
Keegan Jones

Software
Photoshop, Flash, skEdit

Awards
FWA Site Of The Day, Web
Standards Award

Launched
2004

www.brotherjones.com

Technical Advice

Introduction by
Pascal Leroy, group94

04

Technical
Advice

nical

First off, from a technical perspective I don't think there is anything like "the ultimate Ten Commandments of good web design" carved in stone and guarded by holy Internet priests (although, some really show that ambition – but that's another story.) To me there are no golden rules that should be strictly obeyed in order to create a perfect website. But as I've been asked to write this intro, here are some thoughts…

As we all know, the Internet is still a very young discipline and is in constant motion, rapidly evolving over time. Technical boundaries are constantly being pushed back and new rules and insights are often in vogue and rapidly changing. Last year is prehistory in Internet terms. In that regard we have the most exciting job in the world; this is truly a challenging and exciting discipline. No rules, just creative freedom. Well… at least to a certain degree. At all times the web designer will have to keep in mind that ultimately he's creating a technical product… software. Besides being concerned with ergonomics and usability the web designer will have to make sure that this software will need to work exactly as planned (and promised to the client) and that it should keep working over time.

"During production the web designer will devise workarounds for issues that didn't seem to be solvable at first sight. That's the adventurous Lara part: enjoy the music, find the three secrets without getting killed and then proceed to the next level."

I used to say that designing a website is a combination of Lara and Lego. During the creative phase, the challenged web designer will try to push the envelope. Hopefully, he/she will end up with some new insights or at least try out a few new or less obvious concepts. During production the web designer will devise workarounds for issues that didn't seem to be solvable at first sight. That's the adventurous Lara part: enjoy the music, find the three secrets without getting killed and then proceed to the next level.

Not necessarily opposed to this there's the analytic and structured thinking process: Lego stands for proceeding one step at a time and in a logical order. Building a house for instance: basement first, then ground floor and then second floor, finally the roof. Not that Lego is boring, don't get me wrong. I've spent ages with these little colourful blocks, but there's no adventure to be had if you need to remove the roof afterwards because you forgot to add windows, or worse: to have to start all over because the house appears to be too small.

"It's smart to spend enough time on a well thought out plan and to pay attention to all possible issues before hand. In that regard the intelligent web designer will plan his/her project meticulously from a technical point of view and then stick to it."

It's smart to spend enough time on a well thought out plan and to pay attention to all possible issues before hand. In that regard the intelligent web designer will plan his/her project meticulously from a technical point of view and then stick to it. He/she will anticipate the pitfalls; foresee sideways obstacles; design an open structure that will allow possible additional functionality in the future.

Obviously all of the above depends on the complexity and scale of any project. A static five page website using a flat navigational pattern doesn't require much technical analysis in advance. However, a database-driven typography website for instance, like *OurType (see chapter 1, category: Typeface)*, that would allow users to try typefaces and then securely purchase and download single weights or complete font families in one slick Flash environment, and all that managed by the client via a content management system, needs a meticulous project plan. A project plan that would include figuring out the best technical set-up for the planned functionality, organising loading sequences and data retrieval, optimising file architecture and planning transitions, dealing with security and so on.

04 Technical Advice

Prior to any real design activity, any complex project should be fully thought out and described/sketched in so-called "wireframes," which are basically visual skeleton outlines of each page's content and functionality. They will not only help to foresee and anticipate any possible technical bottlenecks but they will also be perfect for helping the customer to understand the project. They will act as excellent guidance for all parties involved during the actual production process.

Conclusion: Good preparation will avoid possible later frustration in every aspect of the project and for everyone involved.

All this sounds boring you might say. I admit that it does. It is indeed so tempting to immediately start drawing pages in Illustrator or Photoshop. And then throw in some Flash or After Effects magic. And then hand it all to the programmers and let them deal with the technical issues. True, that is an option as well.

Pascal Leroy
group94

Bio.
<u>Pascal Leroy</u>
group94

Pascal Leroy is the Founder and Creative Director of group94. Located in Ghent, Belgium, group94 has a diverse and far-reaching client base and portfolio with national and international clients, including the likes of Magnum Photos, Annie Lennox, Lauren Greenfield, Red Bull, and Agfa.

Belgium studio group94 highly acclaimed work covers all business sectors from arts, architecture, media, institutional, scientific, tourism and many more.
–
www.group94.com

"We have the most exciting job in the world; this is truly a challenging and exciting discipline."

Anti-aliased text is text that uses colour variations to make its jagged edges, angles and curves look smoother. On the other side — Aliased text is made by fonts without sub-pixels on curves. Aliased text looks sharp but it has the disadvantage that glyphs (single letters and marks) may lose their definition and look blurred or out of focus when rendered at small sizes. This is especially true with fonts dedicated to Flash and this in turn gave rise to what's known as "pixel" fonts that, when used correctly and at the correct size, render perfectly and crisply.

Do

1
Use aliased text when publishing large amounts of text, like information portals etc.

2
Make sure you put text on whole pixels in Flash and that you use them at their correct size.

3
Use aliased text for small inscriptions when anti-aliased fonts are jagged and unreadable.

Don't

1
Put too many aliased typefaces into your project.

2
Create logotypes based on aliased text. In most cases it doesn't look good.

3
Be careless, make sure every pixel is perfect. There is nothing worse than aliased text when it is blurred or out of focus.

Expert information by
Bartłomiej Rozbicki, Ars Thanea

XRS Nowe Media

Agency
Ars Thanea

Designed by
Bartlomiej Rozbicki

Developed by
Pawel "Magnum"
Piotrzkowski

Software
Flash

Awards
FWA Site Of The Day,
Ultrashock BombShock,
Webesteem Site Of The
Month, ITA, American
Design Award

Launched
2006

www.xrs.pl

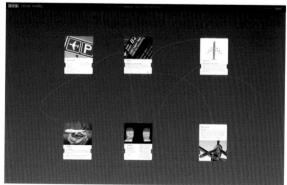

Advertising Agency Heureka

Agency
Sullivan

Designed by
Sullivan

Developed by
Sullivan and Heureka

Software
Flash, Photoshop

Awards
FWA Site Of The Day,
Webstar Festival

Launched
2005

http://en.heureka.pl

Ars Thanea

Agency
Ars Thanea – Bartłomiej
Rozbicki

Designed/Developed by
Bartłomiej Rozbicki

Software
Flash

Awards
FWA Site Of The Day,
Ultrashock BombShock,
Webesteem Site Of The
Month, ITA, American
Design Award

Launched
2003

Mortierbrigade

Agency
group94

Designed/Developed by
group94

Software
FreeHand, Flash, Photoshop,
TopStyle, PHP, MySQL

Awards
FWA Site Of The Day

Launched
2005

www.mortierbrigade.com

The term *computer games* covers a vast range of genres and types from small games for mobile phones to big budget 3D games. There are also online browser-based games, which do not require any installation (you are playing directly in your web browser) and are usually quite easy to play and fast to load. These games are great for short breaks while you are working at your computer.

Browser based games, also known by their related technology as *Flash games* or *Java games*, have become increasingly popular over the years. You can find numerous small games promoting websites, products and services.

Also the Internet has become an excellent place to find some of the more experimental and original games, created quite often by independent developers with very small budgets.

Do

1
Start small.

2
Design your game very carefully in detail before you start.

3
Be original — you cannot beat big development teams and companies with huge resources but you can beat them with new and original ideas.

Don't

1
Imitate or copy.

2
Make it difficult for players to start playing by asking them to register or join.

3
Make it very complicated to understand how to play the game.

Expert information by
Jakub Dvorsky, Amanita Design

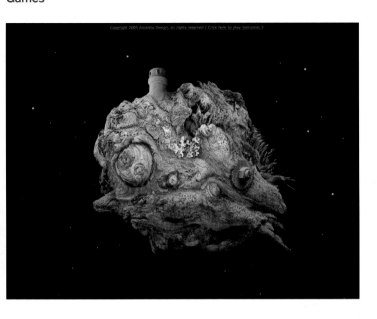

Samorost1
___

Agency
Amanita Design

Designed/Developed by
Jakub Dvorský

Software
Flash, Photoshop

Awards
FWA Site Of The Day,
Webby Award 2004
Nominee, Top Talent Award
2003 Nominee

Launched
2003

http://amanita-design.net/
samorost-1

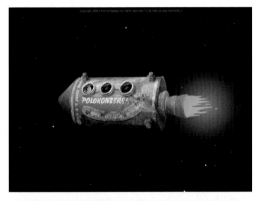

Chiko Accidental Alien

Agency
Indigo digital

Designed by
Nathan Jurevicius, Luke
Jurevicius

Developed by
Grant Camphuisen
– Rhodon IT

Software
Flash

Awards
FWA Site Of The Day,
Australian Game
Developer's Association
– Best PC Game

Launched
2006

www.abc.net.au/chiko

Death in Sakkara

Agency
Preloaded

Designed/Developed by
Preloaded

Software
Flash, Photoshop, Illustrator

Awards
FWA Site Of The Day,
NMA Effectiveness 2006
Entertainment, Flash
Forward 2006 Game, LIA
Finalist, BIMA Finalist,
SXSW Finalist, D&AD
In-book Status

Launched
2005

www.bbc.co.uk/history/
interactive/games/death_
sakkara

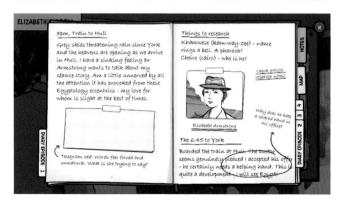

Excellent graphic quality comes with years of experience, attention to detail and a trained eye for image retouch and finalisation.

Fresh designs and illustrations need harmony between the colour palette, the composition, a good choice of photo shoots and well crafted vector illustrations.

Great graphic quality walks hand in hand with style and your own style is the key to making original compositions and really high quality images. Producing work that people look at in awe and wonder who created it is the most rewarding part of graphic design and receiving emails asking about your techniques and style is the highest accolade you can receive.

Do	Don't
1 Have the highest ethics. Always be honest with clients, co-workers and yourself.	**1** Stop learning, finding references or trying to be a better designer.
2 Regularly refresh your knowledge by reading books, surfing the Internet, and keeping up to date with the latest graphic trends, new techniques and software.	**2** Get depressed with negative critics… just try again.
3 Have a good ear to listen to critics, which in turn will make you better.	**3** Don't use comic sans font.

Expert information by
Adhemas Batista, Graphic Designer/Illustrator

Vivagraphics

Agency
Vivagraphics

Designed by
Naoki Izumikawa

Developed by
Vivagraphics

Software
Flash, Photoshop,
Lightwave

Awards
FWA Site Of The Day

Launched
2002

www.viva-graphics.com

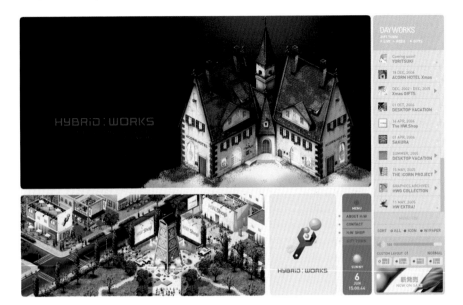

Hybridworks

Agency
Hybridworks Inc.

Designed/Developed by
Masaki Hoshino

Software
Photoshop, Flash

Awards
FWA Site Of The Day, One
Show Interactive 2006
Bronze

Launched
2002

www.hybridworks.jp

I'M SELLING COLORS

I'm Adhemas Batista, a brazilian Art
Director, Graphic Designer and
Illustrator based in Los Angeles CA,
United States. Born in 1980 in the
south of Brazil, São Paulo city, the
biggest metropole of the country.
Married and father of 2 kids, a couple.

This portfolio is a showcase of projects
I have done in the past years. I really
appreciate your visit time. Feel free to
drop me a line if you want.
E-mail: abs@adhemas.com

This website won The Favourite Website of
the Day (TheFWA) in 11 July of 2006

"I'm remembering art of a female people"

About Me

Short Bio

Commercial

ROM Boldie Room
GilyardMFG Website
Logan Renault
KissFM - Kiss Does...
Havaianas Vending Machine
Havaianas Slim
Motion Adrenaline Reel

Havaianas Slim
Motion Adrenaline Reel
Toyota Prius
Botrário Lily Essence
Symantec Folder
Claro MP3
Opis's Website
Havaianas Print Banners
Havaianas Catalogue
Havaianas Website (Update)
Johnnie Walker Red Mix
Artists Play Too
Palm Tree
Havaianas Letters
Havaianas Website
Thai Lounge Buddha
Rapper Kfl's website
Minmo Website

Editorial

Evening Colors
Massive Colors
Skate Colors
30 Colors
Playstation 3
Favorite Colors
Sonorama Exhibition
Smoke Series
Computer Arts Cover
Destructed.info Issue #4
Gamepaused Book
Send Your Style
Destructed.info Issue #7
Select Flavor
Lounge72™ PDF Calendar
Destructed Issue #6
Human? Book
Nanstop Cover Book

Gamepaused Book / Gamepaused

Client Location - Yorkshire / England - 2006
Artwork for the Gamepaused book
My work: Concept and Illustration

Launch

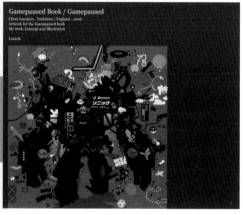

Adhemas.com

Agency
Adhemas Batista
and Pedro Moraes

Designed by
Adhemas Batista

Developed by
Pedro Moraes

Software
Flash

Awards
FWA Site Of The Day

Launched
2006

www.adhemas.com

04 Technical Advice

Havaianas Slim
Motion Adrenaline Reel
Toyota Prius
Botrário Lily Essence
Symantec Folder
Claro MP3
Opis's Website
Havaianas Print Banners
Havaianas Catalogue
Havaianas Website (Update)
Johnnie Walker Red Mix
Artists Play Too
Palm Tree
Havaianas Letters
Havaianas Website
Thai Lounge Buddha
Rapper Kfl's website
Minmo Website

Editorial

Evening Colors
Massive Colors
Skate Colors
30 Colors
Playstation 3
Favorite Colors
Sonorama Exhibition
Smoke Series
Computer Arts Cover
Destructed.info Issue #4
Gamepaused Book
Send Your Style
Destructed.info Issue #7
Select Flavor
Lounge72™ PDF Calendar
Destructed Issue #6
Human? Book
Nanstop Cover Book

The integration of text, image and video can transform a typical website into an immersive experience. Combining new content in a way that allows users to be entertained, while still interacting with the brand, is something that cannot be duplicated in other media.

Integrated content also gives users a choice in the way they receive information about the brand. Do they respond to long-form text, music or animation? Good integrated content marries these channels and lets the user choose a path that's appropriate to their needs, leading to a positive, immersive experience, and more importantly, a positive experience that's unique to your brand.

Do

1
Understand your users and give them a mix of content that is appropriate to them.

2
Allow the user to use different paths to content; give the user access to a non-linear experience.

3
Use content in effective ways, if something can be simply explained with one type of content, do not give them another.

Don't

1
Make the interface too complex — simplicity is the key for users to access integrated content.

2
Have only one size for video content, give the user options.

3
Allow the user only one-way to access information; provide alternatives.

Expert information by
Kelly Kliebe, Saatchi & Saatchi LA

BMW 3 Series

Agency
Fallon

Designed by
Andy Gugel

Developed by
Andy Gugel, Andy LeMay,
Fallon. 3D Rendering: RTT
(Real Time Technologies)

Software
Flash

Awards
FWA Site Of The Day,
Interactive Design Annual
12, One Show Finalist,
Cannes Cyber Lion Finalist

Launched
2005

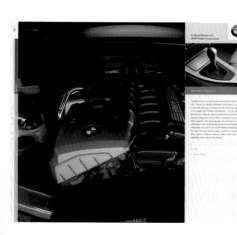

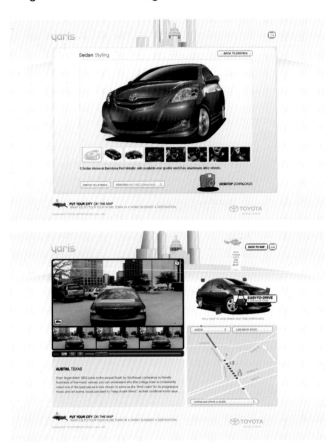

Yaris Digital City Guide

Agency
Saatchi & Saatchi LA

Designed by
Saatchi & Saatchi LA and
Hello Design

Developed by
Hello Design

Software
Photoshop, Illustrator, Flash,
3ds Max, Swift3D, Native
Instruments Kontakt2,
Cameleon5000 synth, GRM
Sound Tools, Waves Plug-
ins, Sorenson Squeeze

Awards
FWA Site Of The Day

Launched
2006

www.toyota.com/vehicles/
minisite/yaris/experience/
index.html

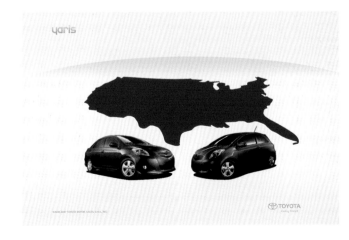

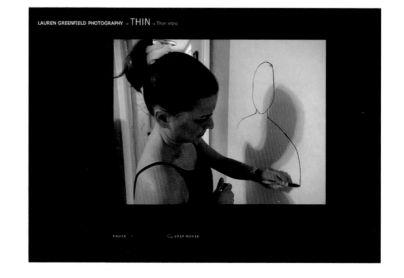

Lauren Greenfield
Photography

Agency
group94

Designed/Developed by
group94

Software
FreeHand, Flash,
Photoshop, TopStyle, Final
Cut Pro, PHP, MySQL

Awards
FWA Site Of The Day

Launched
2006

www.laurengreenfield.com

A multilingual website demonstrates you are able to think, work and deal internationally. If designed properly, it overcomes cultural barriers allowing communication in a native language.

Everyone should think twice about whether or not a multilingual website would be good for them. In a few words, "more languages mean more opportunities."

Do

1
Use professional translation services.

2
Try to have the native language of your business plus English, since this is the most spoken language on the web.

3
Keep language options visible so users will know what's available.

Don't

1
Use translation machines or bots. This could harm your business's reputation.

2
Leave your website in a language other than English without an English translation. If you do half the world won't be able to read your site.

3
Offer language alternatives displayed in your own language. Make sure alternative choices are displayed in their relevant language and maybe with their country's national flag.

Expert information by
Juan Carlos Prieto, Enigmind Ltda.

Pro Vox marketing

Agency
Heavyform

Designed/Developed by
Nenad Bogar

Software
Flash, Photoshop, FreeHand

Awards
FWA Site Of The Day,
GoldenDrum Finalist

Launched
2006

Enigmind

Agency
Enigmind

Designed/Developed by
Juan Carlos Prieto

Software
PHP, MySQL, Flash,
Photoshop

Awards
FWA Site Of The Day, ITA
Site Of The Month

Launched
2006

www.enigmind.com/v1/
welcome.php

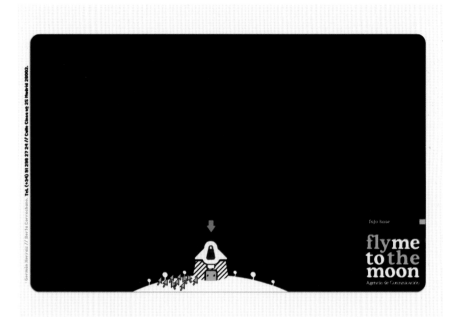

Fly Me to the Moon

Agency
HerraizSoto & Co.

Designed by
Ignasi Tudela

Developed by
Arnau Bosch

Software
FreeHand, Flash, Photoshop

Awards
FWA Site Of The Day, ITA

Launched
2006

www.flymetothemoon.es

In simple terms, a photography archive is an online photo album. It usually consists of two parts: the navigation and the photography presentation.

The navigation is usually a layout of thumbnails, which are small versions of the photographs. There are unlimited possibilities in designing the navigation for a photography archive. Unlike a photography book on your bookshelf, the Internet is interactive and you can do many creative things like spinning the thumbnail, zooming in to take a closer look, or you can upload your own photo to the collection in real time.

The full size photograph is often displayed when a thumbnail is selected. Usually the rest of the screen elements will be dimmed so that users can focus on the selected photograph itself. In many cases, animation and music is helpful to enhance the mood of the experience.

Do

1
Make smart design to display photographs to fit different screen resolutions.

2
Create intuitive navigation. Imitating real movement is always a good idea.

3
Keep the colour and design as neutral as possible so as not to clash with the main focus of the website, the photographs.

Don't

1
Make complicated interfaces, since the photograph itself carries very rich visual content.

2
Load all photographs at the same time; only load a photograph when it's in use or about to be selected.

3
Forget to consider using music to enhance the overall experience.

Expert information by
Henry Chu, pill & pillow

Ashes and Snow

Agency
Critical Mass

Designed/Developed by
Critical Mass

Software
PHP 5, Flash

Awards
FWA Site Of The Day,
Yahoo! Pick Of The Day,
Web Award, ABC News,
DMA

Launched
2006

www.ashesandsnow.org

04 Technical Advice

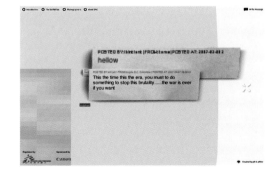

Forgotten War

Agency
pill & pillow

Designed/Developed by
Henry Chu

Software
Flash, PHP, MySQL databse

Awards
FWA Site Of The Day,
London International
Awards

Launched
2006

www.pillandpillow.com/
msfCongo

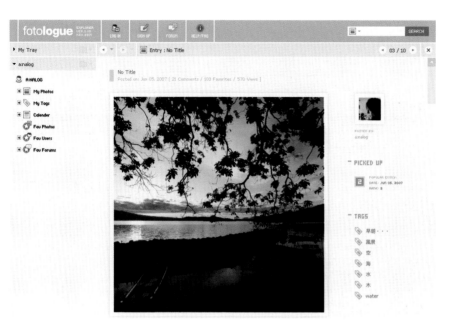

fotologue

Agency
tha ltd.

Designed/Developed by
Yugo Nakamura

Software
Flash

Awards
FWA Site Of The Day

Launched
2006

http://fotologue.jp

Pictures are the first thing a website visitor will look at whilst browsing. They set the standard of the whole site. The average user has an attention span similar to a goldfish... only a few seconds. Thus making the first impression a good one and not compromising on picture quality, is a crucial element to be considered when publishing online.

Do

1
Use correct formats and compression that suits the picture's colour depth, size and transparency.

2
Remove unnecessary noise/ grain if need be.

3
Choose the *Best Quality* option if you use Flash to scale/ rotate pictures.

Don't

1
Compromise quality over file size (within reasonable limits and depending on the type of site).

2
Alter the picture's width/height aspect ratios.

3
Excessively use filters and effects... less is more.

Expert information by
Marcus Wallinder, Meanwhile in nowhere

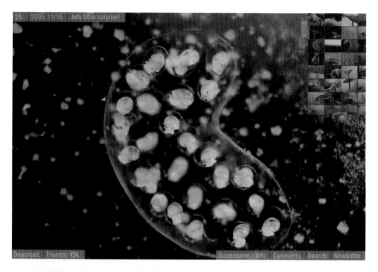

green

Agency
Marcus Wallinder

Designed/Developed by
Marcus Wallinder

Software
Flash

Awards
FWA Site Of The Day, ITA

http://green.colorize.net

Miles Aldridge

Agency
Hi-ReS!

Designed/Developed by
Hi-ReS!

Software
Flash

Awards
FWA Site Of The Day

Launched
2004

www.milesaldridge.com

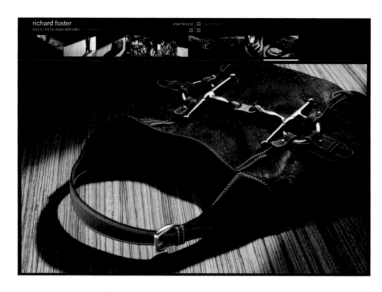

Richard Foster

Agency
group94

Designed/Developed by
group94

Software
FreeHand, Flash,
Photoshop, PHP, MySQL

Awards
FWA Site Of The Day

Launched
2006

www.richardfoster.com

The use of sound in your web project can be instrumental in creating an engaging user experience. It is important to properly prepare and compress the audio content so that a balance is struck between file size and sound quality.

The de facto file format for use in Flash websites is MP3, a compression type that can be customized to suit specific bandwidth needs and limitations. One aspect of the MP3 format that you can customize is the bit rate. This determines the quality at which the audio is compressed, and therefore determines the resulting file size.

Do

1
Edit your sound clips so that there is no wasted silence at the beginning or end of the file.

2
Choose an MP3 bit rate that suits the particular clip. The lower the bit rate the lower the file size, but this also means degraded sound quality.

3
Convert your short sound effects from stereo to mono. Unless you have some heavy panning or spatial effects going on, or if you are including full songs in a project, there's no real need for stereo.

Don't

1
Use bit rates lower than 64Kbps. When dealing with the type of short sound effects and clips one might use for a web interface, there's no real need to compress any further than this.

2
Start with poor quality sound sources. Try to get your audio from a good source, such as a professional sound library or sample CD.

3
Use quiet sound clips. The quieter the sound clip you use, the more the user will have to turn up their speakers to hear.

Expert information by
Scott Hansen, ISO50/Tychomusic

ISO50

Agency
Scott Hansen and Dusty
Brown

Designed by
Scott Hansen

Developed by
Dusty Brown

Software
Photoshop, Flash,
Dreamweaver

Awards
FWA Site Of The Day,
Ultrashock Bombshock, ITA

Launched
2006

http://iso50.com/iso50.html

Using videos to enhance your website's interactive experience is slowly becoming the norm. It is a priority to keep abreast of current technology and know the different methods of delivering video to your site's visitors.

If you want to keep the viewer's interest, videos need to start playing quickly and seamlessly; both options can achieve this.

Generally speaking, streaming allows the user to jump to a specific point in the video without having to download what precedes that point. With progressive loading users can only go as far as what has already loaded.

Choose carefully which of the two options best suits your needs; in Flash, progressive loading tends to let you have more flexibility with what you can do with videos.

Do

1
Have a range of video compressions and sizes to fit the user's bandwidth availability.

2
Choose the lowest frame rate possible for your video. Using 24 fps instead of 30 will help reduce file size.

3
Avoid layering multiple objects (e.g. mask, pngs, and transparent gradients) on top of your Flash video as much as possible for better playback.

Don't

1
Assume that video production/post-production studios know the best ways to output video for the web.

2
Use previously compressed video before converting and compressing for the web.

3
Use interlaced video, as it's meant for traditional television sets and not computer screens.

Expert information by
Christian Ayotte, Sid Lee

MGM Grand

Agency
Sid Lee

Designed by
Philippe Meunier, George
Giampuranis, Nicolas
St-Cyr, Dave Roberts, Fake
Studio – Marc Côté

Developed by
Patrick Matte, Pecunia,
Pierre Paquet, André
Macdonald, Sylvie Tremblay,
Robert Limoges, Steve
Mathieu, Alain Vézina

Software
Photoshop, Flash, After
Effects, Softimage SXI (3D),
Discreet (Autodesk), Flame,
Combustion and Toxik
(Compositing), Microsoft
Framework 2.0, Microsoft
Visual Studio 2005

Awards
FWA Site Of The Month,
2006 Digital Marketing
Award, Boomerang 2006
Best Of Show

Launched
2006

www.mgmgrand.com

Neave.tv

Agency
Paul Neave

Designed/Developed by
Paul Neave

Software
Flash, QuickTime, MySQL, PHP

Awards
FWA Site Of The Day

Launched
2006

www.neave.tv

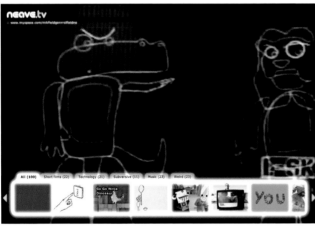

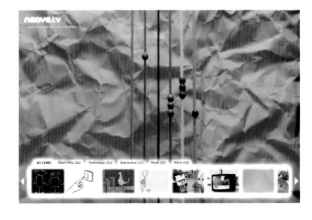

Dear Mr. Barroso

Agency
Forsman & Bodenfors

Designed by
Forsman & Bodenfors

Developed by
Forsman & Bodenfors

Production
B-Reel, Efti

Software
Adobe CS, After Effects,
Flash

Awards
FWA Site Of The Day, Epica,
Eurobest, D&AD

Launched
2006

http://demo.fb.se/e/
systembolaget/dearmrb

Usability is all about the target audience. Knowing who your target audience is and how best to communicate the site objectives to them.

Our approach is very much focused on User Centred Design whereby you address client and end-user requirements at each stage of the development process with usability studies and testing procedures. It ensures that all decisions, such as information architecture, are arrived at as a result of an informed knowledge base.

By allowing this time to plan and test you are able to develop the most appropriate site and provide an end user experience which embodies consistency, discoverability, engagement, information and intuitiveness.

Do

1
Understand your audience.

2
Make use of all features available to enhance the user experience.

Don't

1
Feel bound by typical and common layouts. Clear navigation can be achieved even with an unusual arrangement.

3
Test your developments with the target audience at each stage of the development process.

2
Allow the user to do too much at once.

3
Underestimate the power of planning.

Expert information by
Rob Noble, Lightmaker Group

J.K.Rowling Official Site

Agency
Lightmaker Tunbridge
Wells Ltd

Designed/Developed by
Lightmaker Tunbridge
Wells Ltd

Software
Flash, Photoshop, Illustrator,
3ds Max, Dreamweaver,
Microsoft SQL Server 2000,
Coldfusion MX, Akamai
Edge

Awards
FWA Site Of The Day,
Adobe, MAX Awards 2005
& 2004, Macromedia Site Of
The Day, Eschool Award for
Accessibility, BBC Radio 2
Website of the Day

Launched
2004

www.jkrowling.com

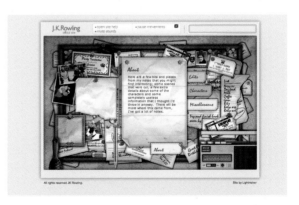

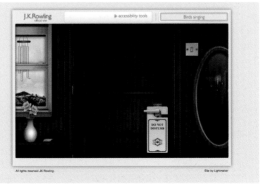

The rapidly increasing implementation of digital videos on the Internet and the growing access to ever higher bandwidths offer a wide range of new opportunities to everyone that produces creative content for this medium. It is especially the visual quality of digital videos that is largely appreciated.

Not only does a high level of visual quality depend on the way in which these videos are technically implemented (compression, frame rate, colour resolution, etc.) but also on more subtle aspects, such as story, message, innovative looks and edits.

In order to take all of these essential parts into account while producing a digital film, you need to thoroughly plan ahead and set objectives to take the right steps at the right time.

Do	Don't
1 Invest a huge amount of time in storyboarding to effectively communicate your vision to all those involved in the project.	**1** Think you can overlook the smaller details just because your final product is to be compressed and probably reduced in size, and don't render CG parts in the low dynamic range.
2 Use high-quality textures and texture filtering in case you are working with CG environments.	**2** Start to think about the musical part at the end of your project.
3 Allow yourself enough time to test different compression schemes and find the best solution to minimise loading time.	**3** Underestimate timings and exhausting workflows. Especially for CG environments, it is crucial to spend enough time to create highly realistic surroundings.

Expert information by
RTT Film-Team, RTT AG

MINI Cooper S with JCW
GP Kit

Agency
Interone Worldwide

Designed by
Mike John Otto, Meike Ufer

Developed by
Michael Ploj, Effekte-Etage

Software
Cinema 4D, Flash,
Photoshop, After Effects

Awards
FWA Site Of The Day, New
York Festivals Gold Medal
2006, Cresta Award 2006

Launched
2005

www.mini.com/gone_fast

Audi R8

Agency
argonauten G2 GmbH

Designed by
Sven Küster, Oliver Hinrichs
(argonautenG2), RTT AG

Developed by
Sven Gessner, Dorian Roy
(argonautenG2), RTT AG

Software
Photoshop, Flash,
Fireworks, After Effects,
Maya, Apple Shake

Awards
FWA People's Choice
Award, FWA Site Of The
Month, German Designer
Club (DDC), Frankfurter
Commerzbank Plaza Site Of
The Year/Silver Megaphone

Launched
2006

http://microsites.audi.com/
audir8/html/index

Stella Artois – L'etranger

Agency
Lowe Tesch

Designed by
Patrik Westerdahl

Developed by
Daniel Isaksson

Software
Flash

Awards
FWA Site Of The Day, Epica

Launched
2006

Content/
Content Management

Introduction by
David Hugh Martin, Fantasy Interactive

05

ent/
Content
Management

When I was asked to write this chapter introduction, I read the title for the first time – "Content and Content Management" – and was immediately horrified. "Wait a minute," I thought. "Content management as in CMS (Content Management System)? Are they really referring to the backend application that our clients use to update their sites? That can't be right, it just can't. I have no idea how they put that together. Why can't they ask a designer to write about design? The cheek of them!"

In reality, content management is not just a backend application. It is a powerful concept, as it delivers the most important thing to the audience: the life, the blood, and the heart of the show… the content.

Of course the Internet is still in its infancy; there are not a lot of perfect examples of nicely presented content. Sometimes I wonder who in the beejeepers knows what the term *content management* actually means. I have a hunch…

As a teenager my bedroom was full of games: Lego, Nintendo, CD singles, toys, clothes, Axe deodorant, and model planes. Sound familiar? Hope so. Naturally, my beloved palace would get messy now and again, but when friends arrived to play Mario Kart on the Super Nintendo, it was suddenly imperative to have an interior that looked like it was magazine-ready. How could I turn the messy room into a cool one, fast? I grabbed everything on the floor, grabbed everything on the shelves, practically grabbed my entire wardrobe and plunked it all on the bed. Within one minute my bedroom would be sparkling, minus what was on the bed. I then had the motivation to place each item on the bed back in its place, one by one, in a pixel perfect formation, always keeping up the standard of a spotlessly clean room which took me just one minute to achieve. With all the stuff on my bed, I could see the content of the room; how much space there was, and what kind of things I had.

"Today, it is imperative to choose the appropriate way to deliver your content to the audience."

I then had a rough idea how long it would take to put it all back in its perfect place. I was motivated, confident, and inspired because I had a holistic view and understanding of what I had to do. My friends were always impressed with my room and how organised I was. Little did they know how it looked five minutes before they arrived!

What in the heck does this have to do with site content? In fact, everything! Before you can comfortably decide how to manage your content, you have to be aware of the content you have and see a clean slate in front of you so you can see where to place that content and how to treat it.

"Today I have a clear instinctive focus to dress up the content appropriately for the site, the client and the target audience. I can feel if a design is 'mature.' I don't mean see, I mean feel — it's something that your instincts tell you."

This chapter will shed light on types of content, such as portals, animation, art, video, music, information and so on. Today, it is imperative to choose the appropriate way to deliver your content to the audience. Over the past nine years, I have personally matured as a designer and creative director. For example, I used to think brushed metal, sci-fi designs with 90 fps motion graphics flying all around the place was cool. Back then it was the bomb, and made Fantasy Interactive in the early days of Flash. Today I have a clear instinctive focus to dress up the content appropriately for the site, the client and the target audience. I can feel if a design is "mature." I don't mean see, I mean feel — it's something that your instincts tell you. I know when designing portals exactly how fast the drop-down should drop and when to use a fade and when not to. I put usability first, and use design and animation to make usability the most fashionable challenge in our business. With so much content on today's sites and no uniform usability standards that today's average user recognises, managing your content includes understanding your audience.

The tools we use today for displaying frontend content are primarily Flash. It's flexible and powerful. We haven't completely harnessed it yet. Nobody has. Flash gives us a huge opportunity to fail but when it succeeds the results are staggering. There are thousands of *dos* and *don'ts*, but as a rule of thumb it's important to balance your content. What does that mean? Organisation and carefully choosing the amount of content to display at once is important. Layout and font choices are crucial to legibility. What the user should focus on first, second and third is absolutely your responsibility.

Introduction

"It is essential, when developing the web from a bird's eye perspective, to understand the scope of the content, the space in which you have to work with, and the way in which you want the content to read."

The majority of content on anything we design today is text. Text! Text! Text! Text! It's boring and is the culprit for making the majority of today's websites look like they were made before *Yahoo.com* saw the light of day. You must treat your text and how you present it as the heart of your content. Animation, sound effects, videos and music will have no impact if the user doesn't understand what they are looking at. They do not respect their experience. How to go from one piece of content to the next is the job of navigation, which is often an afterthought, and is thus poorly executed. If the user is not comfortable with the navigation system, chances are they will not see your gloriously designed content.

Clearly, the clarity of the content should be clear to the audience. You see how muddy text can be.

It is essential, when developing the web from a bird's eye perspective, to understand the scope of the content, the space in which you have to work with, and the way in which you want the content to read. Then, be a manager and appropriately manage your content!

David Hugh Martin
Fantasy Interactive

Bio.
<u>David Hugh Martin</u>
Fantasy Interactive

David Hugh Martin founded
Fantasy Interactive on the
principles of quality over
quantity, which still forefronts
the company's success today.
The only two times FWA Site
Of The Year Winner, David
plays the key role in FI's
creative and design offerings.
FI has developed into a
unique interactive player in
the industry that caters for the
world's largest clients.

Fantasy Interactive was
recently recognised as one of
the most financially successful
and growing companies in
Sweden when David received
the Supergasell award from
Sweden's Minister of Trade.
David has been featured in
numerous books, newspapers
and magazines globally.
–
www.f-i.com

"What the user should focus on first, second and third is absolutely your responsibility."

Animation is the art of creating an illusion of movement through a sequence of images. This "artificial" movement "tricks" our brain into believing the imagery, which is why we, as children and even now as adults, will always be intrigued and fascinated by animation.

There are various types of animation techniques as well as mediums used. The more common forms are traditional cel animation, stop/clay animation, 3D/computer animation and more recently and also relevant to this book, online Flash/GIF animation.

Animation plays a key role in the online medium. It helps breathe life into a website, gives it character and in doing so, creates a much more engaging user experience.

Do

1
Keep the animated sequences short and sweet.

2
Inject some humour, be creative and put in some surprises for the user to discover.

3
Add interaction to the animated subject and sync it with appropriate music and sound effects.

Don't

1
Get too carried away (watch the file size) or excessively use bitmaps if vectors will do.

2
Interfere with navigational aspects of the site or it will become frustrating for the user.

3
Forget to include a *Skip* function if the animation is too long and don't loop music if it's only a few seconds in length or forget a *Sound Off* button.

Expert information by
Sean Lam, Kinetic Singapore

Wangfan Network

Agency
Wangfan Network

Designed by
Idea Prisoner

Developed by
Wally Ho, Rex Tan

Software
Photoshop, Flash, Eclipse,
Visual Studio, SQL Server

Awards
FWA Site Of The Day

Launched
2006

www.wangfan.com

Corpse Bride

Agency
Blitz

Designed by
Ken Martin, Mark Cohn

Developed by
Ivan Todorov

Software
Photoshop, Flash, 3ds Max,
Maya

Awards
FWA Site Of The Month,
Los Angeles Addy
Awards, District 15 Addy
Awards, Adobe Site of the
Day Award, Hollywood
Reporter Key Art, London
International Advertising
Award

Launched
2005

www.corpsebridemovie.com

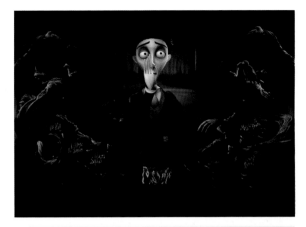

Kinetic Singapore

Agency
Kinetic Singapore

Designed/Developed by
Sean Lam

Software
Flash, Audition, Photoshop,
Dreamweaver

Awards
FWA Site Of The Day,
D&AD Awards, Clio Awards,
One Show Interactive,
Asia Interactive Award,
Singapore Creative Circle
Awards

Launched
2005

www.kinetic.com.sg

05 Content/Content Management

An illustration is a graphic representation designed to support a message, provide instruction, evoke emotion in the viewer.

From the cave paintings of early man, to the illuminated manuscripts of medieval monks, to its Golden Age in the early 20th century, illustration is one of the oldest and most successful forms of communication. It would be impossible to find a vein of modern media today that doesn't take advantage of illustration's versatility.

It is a medium unbound by the real world limitations of photography, broader in its capacity to communicate visual ideas than language. It is a medium limited only by the illustrator's skill and imagination.

Do

1
Give the illustration a context to allow the viewer to understand how and where it is used.

2
Display the illustration as large and clearly as possible.

3
Provide technical details such as the medium you used, the dimensions, and the paper/surface you created on.

Don't

1
Hide your work behind confusing navigation or extensive animated introductions.

2
Include work you're not confident is your best work.

3
Try to cater to an audience. Put the work you like out there, and let the audience find you.

Expert information by
Kevin Cornell, Bearskinrug

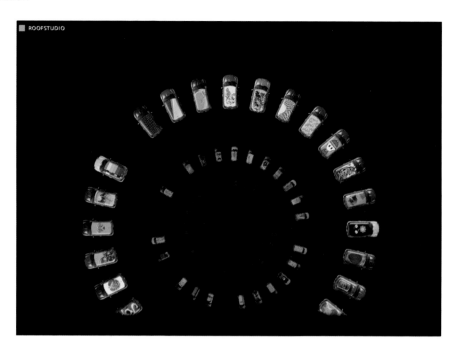

Roof Studio

Agency
Crispin, Porter + Bogusky

Designed by
Alex Bogusky, Andrew
Keller, Jeff Benjamin, Rahul
Panchal, Trisha Ting, Brian
Tierney, Jackie Hathiramani

Developed by
EVB and Beam Interactive

Software
Flash

Awards
FWA Site Of The Day,
ANDYs, Yahoo! Big
Idea Chair, One Show,
Webby Nominee, Cannes
2006 Cyber Finalist,
Communication Arts
Interactive, ID Magazine

Launched
2005

www.roofstudio.com

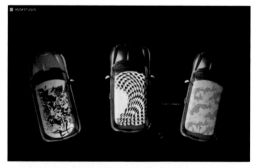

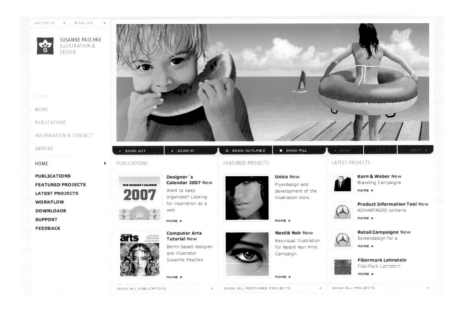

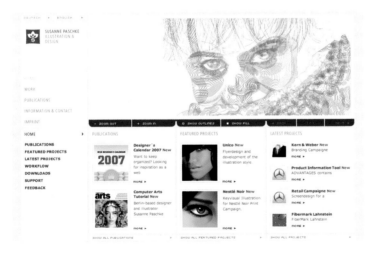

Susanne Paschke

Agency
Susanne Paschke

Designed by
Susanne Paschke

Developed by
Susanne Paschke, Stephan
Schulz, Marcel Eichner

Software
Photoshop

Awards
FWA Site Of The Day

Launched
2006

www.susannepaschke.de

The Bearskinrug
Sketchbook

Agency
Kevin Cornell

Designed/Developed by
Kevin Cornell

Software
Flash

Awards
FWA Site Of The Day

Launched
2003

www.bearskinrug.co.uk/
_work/sketchbook1/launch

The one aspect of the web as a mass media that sets it most apart from all others is its ability to facilitate communication.

As human beings we have an instinctive desire and need to connect with others and share our thoughts, opinions and knowledge. Some sites strive to communicate, provide service or entertain but the sites that truly transcend, to a point of relevance, are those that are able to build and sustain a community of users that interact with each other. Web 2.0 is just a natural embracing of this fact and a mindset to guide the design and implementation of content experiences that empower community.

Do

1
Find a platform of content or culture that can be the basis of your community, for example, what photos are to Flickr.

2
Find unique ways in which users can personally express themselves.

3
Build in tools that allow users to take content with them to other personal pages or blogs.

Don't

1
Expect your concept to appeal to everyone; you need to connect in specific ways not general ways to a culture of users.

2
Make your site difficult or tedious to use.

3
Be concerned about legal usage rights; fear of being sued would have kept Blogger, Flickr, MySpace, YouTube and so many others from ever happening.

Expert information by
Todd Purgason, JUXT Interactive

Globulos

Agency
GlobZ

Designed by
Laurent Fernandez

Developed by
Fabien Riffaud

Software
Flash

Awards
FWA Site Of The Day,
Flash Festival in France
(2003): People's Choice,
Flash Film Festival New
York City 2003

Launched
2003

www.globulos.com

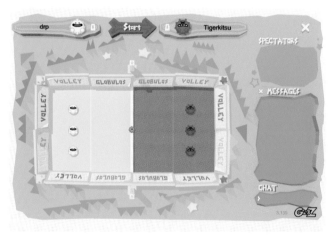

Creating a site that delivers a heavy amount of information is both a blessing and a curse. You, as an interface designer, have to be very careful not to overwhelm the layout and keep a clear path to help steer guests to the information they are most interested in. The good news about having a lot of content to deliver is that you have an arsenal of things to keep the site interesting, diverse and alive. Use it to your advantage.

You don't have to see everything at once. Remember that your audience is intelligent and they also have individual tastes. Welcome your visitors. Let them know there is a lot to see and give them an easy way to explore the direction they are most interested in. This way you set them off on the right path.

Ensure that there is an easy way to get an idea of all that the site has to offer. This, in most cases, can be handled with a clearly stated site map. People like to know what areas are available and if they may have missed anything that might hold more interest to them.

Do

1
Provide clear
navigation.

2
Allow room to explore.

3
Keep it interesting
around every bend.

Don't

1
Overload the layout.

2
Complicate the
message.

3
Lose focus of what
is important to your
audience.

Expert information by
Will Weyer, Wiretree

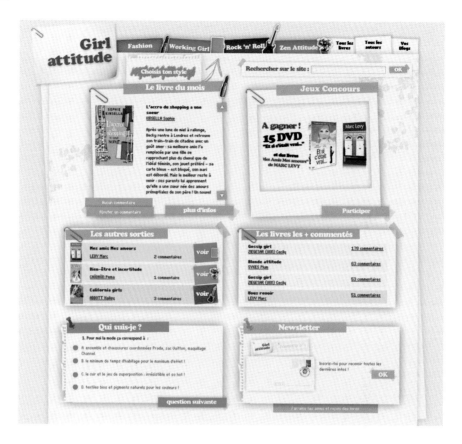

Girl Attitude

Agency
Soleil Noir

Designed/Developed by
Soleil Noir

Software
Flash, Photoshop

Awards
FWA Site Of The Day

Launched
2006

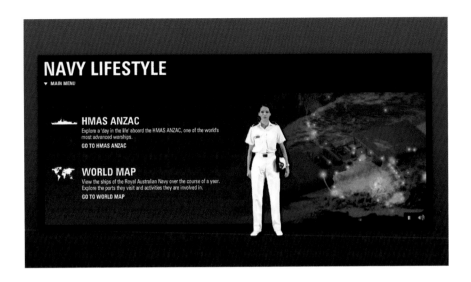

Navy Lifestyle

Agency
Visual Jazz

Designed by
Brett White, Dave Budge,
Justin Arthur

Developed by
Steven Woolcock

Software
Flash, Photoshop, 3ds Max,
Final Cut Pro

Awards
FWA Site of the Day,
IAB Creative Showcase

Launched
2006

http://navylifestyle.
defencejobs.gov.au

If you're looking to launch a career in music, film, video games, design, or animation, you've come to the right place. Over the past 28 years, Full Sail Real World Education has built a reputation as one of the premier media arts colleges in the world. Throughout the entertainment industry, Full Sail graduates have made their names working on award-winning films and albums, acclaimed video games and design projects, live productions, and more.

Full Sail's Master's, Bachelor's, and Associate's Degrees for creative minds include Computer Animation, Digital Arts & Design, Entertainment Business, Film, Game Development, Graphic Design, Music Business, Recording Arts, and Show Production & Touring. Regardless of which program at our school you choose, one of Full Sail's fundamental goals is to encourage the union of art and technology. Pick a degree program to come inside and learn more.

Low-Bandwidth Site

Enter

» Request More Information

Full Sail

Agency
Wiretree

Designed by
Will Weyer, Craig Daily

Developed by
Jeff Askew

Software
Flash, Cold Fusion, Photoshop, Cinema 4D, After Effects, Audition, Illustrator, Sorenson Squeeze

Awards
FWA Site of the Day, W3 Awards (Gold)

Launched
2006

Let's face it — being a rock star and being a web designer is practically the same thing. Put your little hand in mine, dear reader, and allow me to tell you a few things you should keep in mind when creating a site for a musician…

Do

1
Inject humour. I think humour is key to anything really (websites too).

2
Make them sing and dance on their website. Remember… they are rock stars!

3
Whatever you want. For God's sake, you're making a site for the Rolling Stones!

Don't

1
Try and steal the rock star's girlfriend. When I said being a rock star and being a web designer was the same thing earlier, I was kidding.

2
Listen to input from the rock star. You can nod your head and say "okay, okay Keith, now you go off with your guitars."

3
Work through a large advertising agency if you care even a little about how the site will turn out. Insist on a direct line of communication with the musician (or at least their #1 handler/P.A.).

Expert information by
Jordan Stone, sofake

Beck

Agency
Hi-ReS!

Designed/Developed by
Hi-ReS!

Software
Flash

Awards
FWA Site Of The Day

Launched
2005

http://archive.hi-res.net/
beck

Agency
sofake

Designed/Developed by
Jordan Stone

Software
Photoshop, Flash

Awards
FWA Site Of The Month,
SXSW

Launched
2004

www.billyharveymusic.com

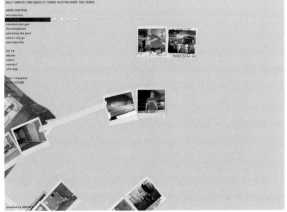

Yulia Nau

Agency
Wireframe Studio

Designed/Developed by
Andries Odendaal

Software
Photoshop, Flash

Awards
FWA Site Of The Month, Loerie Award, Construction New Media Award (South Africa), Stone Award (South Africa)

Launched
2002

http://www.wireframe.
co.za/yulia/eng.htm

A Killer Portal is a perfect balance between design, technology and content. There are few to zero examples of next generation portals as the technology and demand for them has just begun. Flash and also Flex enables us to develop very fast, engaging and flexible portals that cater for rich media content and the sky is the limit for design.

However, such an undertaking can be a killer project for your team or company if one side fails. You can have an impact on millions of users daily, so usability is a key factor and balance is imperative.

Do

1
Access the content very carefully that will populate the portal. Categorize it into media types and evaluate the basics such as the size of images, videos and the amount of text that accompanies a news story.

2
Remember that content is king, so facilitate for it.

3
Take a breather and step back once in a while. Look at how far you have come and if you want to make a change, make it now.

Don't

1
Ever under-estimate usability.

2
Let technology rule design or design rule technology.

3
Underestimate the importance of communication within your team.

Expert information by
David Hugh Martin, Fantasy Interactive

The FWA:
Favourite Website Awards

Agency
Jason Hickner and Nathan
Young

Designed by
Nathan Young

Developed by
Jason Hickner

Software
Flash

Awards
Yahoo! Pick Of The Day, Adobe
UK Showcase, Macromedia
Site Of The Day, Ultrashock
Bombshock

Launched
2005

www.thefwa.com

Momentum Pictures

Agency
Franki&Jonny

Designed by
Franki Goodwin

Developed by
Jonny Green

Software
Flash, Photoshop, TextMate,
Ruby-on-Rails

Awards
FWA Site Of The Day

Launched
2006

www.momentumpictures.
co.uk

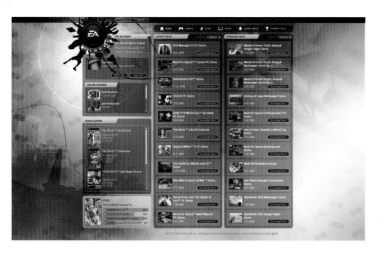

Agency
Electronic Arts

Designed by
Liam McCallum

Developed by
Joel Beencke

Software
Photoshop, Flash,
Dreamweaver, Fireworks

Awards
FWA Site of the Day

Launched
2006

www.ea.co.nz

Road Runner

Agency
Fantasy Interactive

Designed by
David Hugh Martin

Developed by
Christopher Marsh and
Noah Paci (RR), Bjarne
Erkensjo, Jonas Eliasson,
and Andreas Enqvist (FI)

Software
Photoshop, Flash, Maya

Awards
FWA Site Of The Year,
Site Of The Month,
Site Of The Day,
Ultrashock Bombshock

Launched
2004

Showreels and motion graphics are website features that offer great opportunities for personalisation and interaction, and if used properly, these features can present your company at the very highest level.

Showreels can consist of individual motion picture/video projects, as well as montages. In using showreels, it is important to note that, while offering the individual projects or montages may produce the desired results, the context in which those pieces are featured is a crucial branding environment, where you have a key opportunity to connect yourself, your company and/or your brand with the work being presented.

In my own experience, I find that the use of motion graphics should be viewed as an opportunity to creatively extend a company's identity through its website.

Do	Don't
1 Pick a musical track from the right genre that speaks to your audience, which is upbeat in terms of bpm and in overall tone.	**1** Put work on your showreel that's not truly strong; if spots one, two and three are good, but number 4 is just so-so, stick with the good stuff and don't show too much work, because no one will sit through it.
2 Ensure that you encode your materials properly, that you have a good audio mix and levels, that the project loads quickly, looks good while playing back online, and plays properly in all browsers on all platforms.	**2** Post work that isn't "ownable" by you or your company.
3 Find a viable reason or idea relating to key characteristics of your company before exploring the use of motion graphics in your website.	**3** Incorporate motion graphics just for the sake of having something move on your website; if used for no apparent reason, using motion graphics can work against you.

Expert information by
Jake Banks, Stardust Studios

adidas Originals

Agency
Neue Digitale

Designed by
Bejadin Selimi

Developed by
Jens Steffen

Software
Flash

Awards
FWA Site Of The Day,
Cannes Cyber Lion Silver,
New York Festivals,
CRESTA 2005 Grand Prix,
Eurobest Award Gold, ADC
Germany 2006 Bronze, The
One Show Interactive 2006
Silver, Clio Awards Bronze,
D&AD Award 2006 Bronze

Launched
2005

www.neue-digitale.de/
projects/originals_ss2005

Stardust Studios

Agency
Stardust Studios

Designed by
Jake Banks

Developed by
Joshua Davis

Software
Flash

Awards
FWA Site Of The Day,
Tween Best Reel

Launched
2005

http://www.stardust.tv

Nike Air

Agency
Big Spaceship

Designed/Developed by
Big Spaceship

Software
Flash

Awards
FWA Site Of The Month

Launched
2006

http://archive.bigspaceship.com/nikeair

A footstep, a breath and the "click" of your mouse produce sound. Our ears anticipate sound as a natural indicator of most actions we perform. Why, then, shouldn't it be natural for a website to respond with sound as we use it?

Web pages are moving from being mute papers to becoming rich multimedia pieces. Sound can bring alive the metaphor a website represents. It can add thrill, mood, understanding and meaning, turning that mute paper into a first-class experience.

Use sound with special care and sense, balance it with silence, and consider cautiously the web audience it is targeted to.

Do	Don't
1 Think of sound as a design element. Blend a common "style" to the different sounds in your site and try to be consistent, as you would do with the visual style.	**1** Go crazy. Unsolicited sound or loud music can be irritating.
2 Remember that event sounds, triggered by specific user actions, should be meaningful and consistent so the user can relate them to the actual activities being performed.	**2** Present content using speech without providing an alternative text form or description.
3 Always provide a visible option to turn sound off and make sure it works!	**3** Overtrust your sound editing skills. Being a great designer or developer doesn't mean you are an audio pro too!

Expert information by
Jorge Hernández, Wunderman Copenhagen

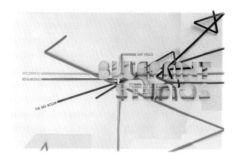

Blueprint Studios

Agency
magneticNorth

Designed by
Suzie Webb

Developed by
Paul Neave

Software
Flash

Awards
FWA Site Of The Day,
Design Week Awards 2006
Information Website Winner,
Roses Design Awards 2006
Silver, Adobe Y-Design
Awards 2006 Interactive
Design Finalist; BIMA
Awards 2006 B2B Finalist

Launched
2005

www.blueprint-studios.com

05 Content/Content Management

Sports websites need equal parts inspiration and innovation. Creating new experiences that capture and engage the consumer is a significant mission. Leading brands often provide a platform of amazing stories and relevance to a broad range of consumers. This should be seen as both an opportunity and a tremendous challenge. One has to factor in the amount of noise – the sheer amount of interactive entertainment – around the sports-minded, fashion-leading, and technology-inclined consumer. Competing for a good share of that consumer's attention is sometimes comparable to some of the greatest battles we've seen in the history of sport itself.

Do

1
Make the product king. Experiment in new ways to showcase the product.

2
Remember a picture is worth a thousand words. Video is worth a million.

3
Spend time understanding your consumers, stay true to your audience, and if you think you're taking yourself too seriously, you probably are.

Don't

1
Forget to communicate a story.

2
Tell too many messages at the same time. Don't try to be all things to all people.

3
Think that just because you can, you should.

Expert information by
Marcus Ericsson, Creative Director/Photographer

Jordan Brand

Agency
Blast Radius

Designed by
Marcus Ericsson

Developed by
Steve Bond

Software
Flash

Awards
FWA Site Of The Month,
Digital Marketing Awards,
GDC Design Awards,
Communication Arts Design
Annual, Clio Interactive
Awards, One Show, Flash in
the Can, Cannes Lions, ADC
Canada, Web Awards

Launched
2005

www.jumpman23.com

UFC 66

Agency
Red Interactive Agency

Designed by
Jared Kroff, Adam
DeVincent

Developed by
Jared Kroff, Adam
DeVincent

Software
Photoshop, Flash

Awards
FWA Site Of The Day

Launched
2006

http://66.ufc.com

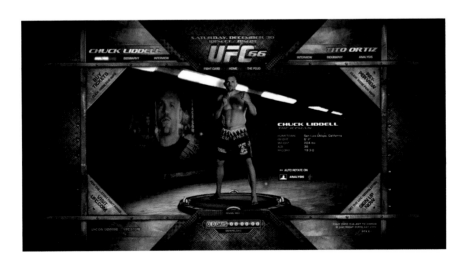

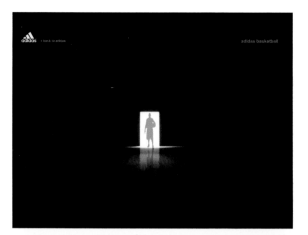

Agency
EVB

Designed by
Jason Zada

Developed by
Biko Allen, Josh Sullivan

Software
Flash, After Effects

Awards
FWA Site Of The Day,
Summit, Horizon, San
Francsisco Addy Awards
Best In Division, Internet
Advertising Competition,
Clios, One Show, London
International Awards

Launched
2006

05 Content/Content Management

From the moment the Internet became realized as a new form of information distribution in the mid 1990s, the greatest challenge for brands and developers alike has been transforming video, as we know it, over to this new interactive medium.

With broadband penetration at an all-time high worldwide, video is starting to have an amazing impact on the web. We have all seen the latest interactive examples showcasing long-form video content and creative interactive interpretation of video through Flash. Over the next decade, I believe we will see an even more innovative period where our industry will take interactive video to creative highs — both on and off the web.

Do	Don't
1 Remember that when shooting any video (even for the web) it is always important to storyboard what you plan to shoot.	**1** Expect a consumer to wait for a video file size that is abnormally high. Use streaming and content delivery methods whenever possible.
2 Bear in mind that short takes are better suited for interactivity especially when used as part of a design element on a site.	**2** Film your subjects against colourful backgrounds if it's not necessary.
3 Note compression times and usability factors when shooting video for the web — the longer the take, the longer the load.	**3** Forget to plan. It is easy to get fooled into thinking you can just shoot and compress video but if you do not plan, you'll be wasting time.

Expert information by
Matthew Szymczyk, Zugara

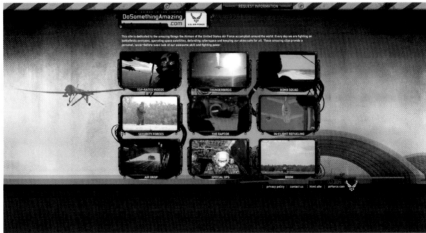

Do Something Amazing

Agency
Zugara

Designed/Developed by
Zugara

Software
Flash

Awards
FWA Site Of The Day,
Adcritic Pick Of The Week

Launched
2006

www.dosomethingamazing.
com

Wolfboys

Agency
Sid Lee

Designed by
Philippe Meunier, Nicolas
St-Cyr, Jonathan Rosman,
Louis-Philippe Riel, Quatre
Zéro Un, Yan Turgeon,
Claudia Roy, Richard Jean-
Baptiste, La Majeure

Developed by
Christian Ayotte, Patrick
Matte, Claude Beauchemin,
Robert Limoges

Software
Photoshop, Flash, After
Effects, Final Cut Pro

Awards
FWA Site Of The Day

Launched
2006

Move Me

Agency
Amberfly

Designed by
Peter Barr

Developed by
Douglas Noble

Software
Flash, Photoshop,
Dreamweaver, PHP, MySQL

Awards
FWA Site Of The Day, ITA,
Netscape Cool Site Of
The Day, American Design
Award

Launched
2006

www.move-me.com

Loft Halloween Show!

Agency
Junichi Kato

Designed/Developed by
Junichi Kato

Software
Flash

Awards
FWA Site Of The Day

Launched
2006

http://cmd9.com/portfolio/
loft2006

E-Commerce

Introduction by
Mark Ferdman, Freedom Interactive Design

06

Commerce: the trading of something of economic value such as goods, services, information or money between two or more entities. Its origins began in prehistoric times at the spark of human communications. People began to barter with each other. It's fascinating modern history has evolved over nearly 900 years, from the first European trading guild in 1157, to the opening of the spice trade in 1498, to the founding of the Dutch East India Company in 1602, and all the way up to the creation of the World Trade Organization and the launch of *Amazon.com*, both in 1995.

The Marketplace: buyers and sellers carry out their business, and the gears of capitalism are greased. Today, the growing influence of the Internet has enabled the formation of new, powerful, and exciting types of electronic commerce. Innovative and sophisticated marketers are setting themselves apart from their competition.

So what makes a website excel in the commercial field? Many of the same things that make businesses successful offline – clear communication, top-shelf customer service, innovative presentation, a strong brand identity, sometimes sex appeal, sometimes shock appeal, and sometimes the element of surprise. High-quality products or services create demand. An entertaining, easy-to-use presentation and a simple method to complete a purchase, seals the deal.

> **"Well-known brands entertain us with funky animations and one-act plays that re-invent traditional product catalogs."**

There is no better place to get a comprehensive overview of the best of breed in online commerce than Favourite Website Awards. This chapter contains a diverse group of examples.

Well-known brands like Converse and IKEA entertain us with funky animations and one-act plays that re-invent traditional product catalogs. Converse Russia's site seems as much a tip of the cap to Monty Python, Ralph Steadman, and Peter Max as to the Chuck Taylor All-Star basketball shoes that it promotes. IKEA's *Come into the Closet* site is chock full of complex set designs, an original musical score, diverse characters, and a refreshing sense of humour.

When it comes to customer service, Borders has done a fantastic job with its holiday gift websites. The *Giftmixer* website was an early adapter of user-initiated database mining, disguised behind a slick interface and one of the first of its kind. The *Season of Surprises* site takes it a step further by expanding on the metaphor with a children's paper doll cut out design that makes for a fun, totally personalized experience. The results are targeted product recommendations that lead to increased sales.

"Push the boundaries of your imagination with groundbreaking ideas. Bust out of the box and have fun."

Websites like *Shop Composition* and *Uniqlo* contain innovative presentations that merchandise their wares in ways that capture attention and keep it. *Shop Composition*'s stylish and colourful images load and pop before your eyes. *Uniqlo*'s super-creative art piece is simply amazing. Kalle's squeeze-tube caviar site has a kitschy retro feel that works. Our own *Would You Like a Website?* puts a modern twist on a 20th century sidewalk phenomenon – the sandwich board salesman.

There are many things to consider when planning, designing, and developing a commercial website. These include an audit of your audience, brand assets, budget, timeline, and available technologies. Most importantly, you'll need to enlist a talented and capable team. Your designers and developers must collaborate from the onset of the project, because design and technology go hand in hand.

Utilise cutting edge software like Photoshop, After Effects and Flash to create amazing animations and motion graphics. Integrate front-end designs with secure and robust database applications that connect your website to customers and enable you to foster personalized, one-on-one relationships with them. Push the boundaries of your imagination with ground-breaking ideas.

Bust out of the box and have fun.

"The growing influence of the Internet has enabled the formation of new, powerful, and exciting types of electronic commerce."

Bio.
Mark Ferdman
Freedom Interactive Design

Mark Ferdman is Founder and Creative Director of Freedom Interactive, located in New York City. Since 1997 he has overseen the design and development for hundreds of high-profile digital design projects. Mark's clients have included Crispin, Porter + Bogusky, Fox Searchlight, Goodby, Silverstein & Partners, Kellogg's, L'Oréal, MGM, and Universal Pictures, amongst dozens of others.

He lives in suburban New York with his wife Joanna and two young daughters, Zoe and Charlie.
–
freedominteractivedesign.com

As opposed to simply offering the user a page of products where they can click and purchase, we should strive to create an experience that offers products and services catered to that individual user. To achieve this, you have to get certain information about that user.

The first step should be to create an emotional connection with the user through the interactive experience you are building. You will also need to develop a strategy where you can take the boring process of a questionnaire, and turn it into an entertaining journey that the user has fun participating in.

The end goal is to gain information about the user in order to customise their buying experience. Instead of having pages of products to sort through, the user will be much more inclined to make a purchase if they are choosing between items that have some relevance to them.

Do

1
Create an emotional connection with the user — they need to care about why they are there, or they won't stay.

2
Keep the product or service you are selling in mind as you create the experience around the point of purchase.

3
Devise a strategy that allows you to access information about the user so you can suggest products for them to buy.

Don't

1
Use long questionnaires or surveys to gain information from the user.

2
Create an engaging experience that is too long. Remember, your goal is to engage the user and then make a sale.

3
Force the user to purchase certain products — the key is to get information, then make subtle suggestions that guide them in their purchase.

Expert information by
Dan LaCivita, Firstborn

Season of Surprises

Agency
Firstborn

Designed/Developed by
Firstborn

Software
Flash, XML, .NET C#, MS
SQL Server 2000 Database

Awards
FWA Site Of The Day

Launched
2005

www.fborn.com/websites/
144_seasonofsurprises

06 E-Commerce

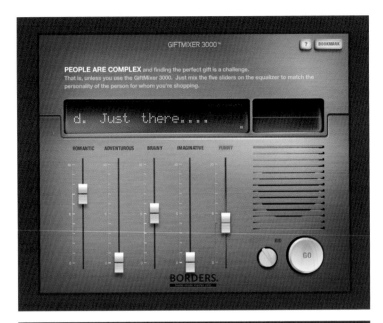

Giftmixer 3000

Agency
Firstborn

Designed/Developed by
Firstborn

Software
Flash, ASP Classic,
MS SQL Server 2000
Database, WebTrends
Metrics Tracking, Akamai
Optimization

Awards
FWA Site Of The Day,
Communication Arts, One
Show, Clio, Andy Award

Launched
2004

www.fborn.com/
websites/106_borders_
giftMixer

Behr Paint and Wood Stain

Agency
Arc Worldwide USA

Designed/Developed by
Arc Worldwide USA

Software
Flash, Photoshop, Illustrator,
3ds Max, After Effects

Awards
Laslo, Creative Suite

Launched
2004

www.behr.com

The shopping cart is the most important aspect of any e-commerce site. It functions as the shop window for an online retailer and as such, needs to be capable of displaying products in the best possible light. It can instil confidence and increase online purchases, or it can put potential customers off using a site altogether.

Before developing a shopping cart, think carefully about what you are trying to achieve and consider how a potential customer would use it and what their expectations are. Research other sites that sell similar products and evaluate what works and what doesn't about their carts.

Do

1
Keep it simple. Customers need to feel comfortable with a cart as soon as possible, or they will be discouraged from browsing through the products on offer.

2
Use terms web users are used to, such as *Add to Order* or *View Basket*. Deviating too far from these standards can confuse potential customers.

3
Know your customers. Find out what they're expecting from the shopping cart and respond to that.

Don't

1
Overload customers with choices too soon. Concentrate on making products easier to find by improving the navigation, not by displaying them all on the first page of the cart.

2
Hide from customers. Make it easy for them to ask questions, it will give them confidence in the site and its ability to deliver.

3
Forget that a shopping cart is just the beginning. A successful online retailer will spend as much time developing the backend of the shopping experience.

Expert information by
James Down, De Facto Design

Storyville

Agency
Wiretree

Designed by
Will Weyer

Developed by
Jeff Askew, Robb Bennett,
Ryan Taylor

Software
Flash, Photoshop, 3DS
Max, After Effects, Audition,
Illustrator, Sorenson
Squeeze

Awards
FWA Site of the Day

Launched
2006

www.storyville.com

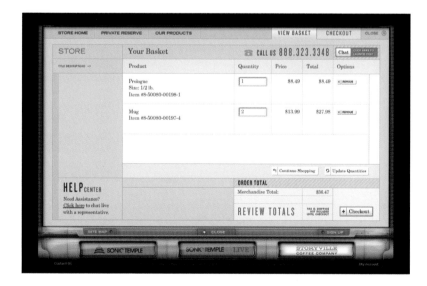

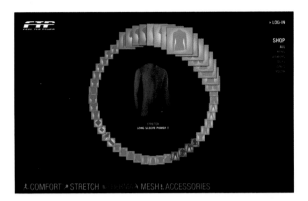

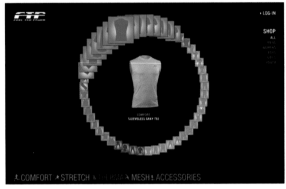

Feel The Power

Agency
Freedom Interactive

Designed by
Matt Sundstrom

Developed by
Shea Gonyo

Software
Flash, SQL Server, XML

Awards
FWA Site Of The Day,
Flash in the Can
e-Commerce

Launched
2005

www.feelthepower.biz

Fred Perry

Agency
De Facto Design

Designed by
James Daly, Tom Stimpson

Developed by
James Down

Software
Flash, Photoshop,
Bare Bones BBedit

Awards
FWA Site of the Day

Launched
2001

www.fredperry.com

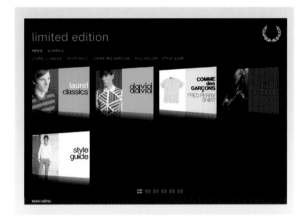

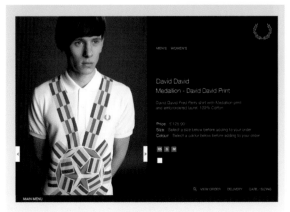

267

A corporate website can often be the source of a company's information as well as becoming the heart and soul of each company. It's a place to present a company to a global audience and will usually include the company overview, philosophy, history and management.

Corporate websites do not have to be boring static places, they can be creative and innovative and show a company's forward thinking attitudes and outlook. They are also an excellent opportunity for self-promotion.

Do	Don't
1 Add a table of contents and, if possible a search engine to provide a good overview and easy access to information.	**1** Publish any secrets.
2 Make allowances for different target groups (customers, media, investor relations, recruitment etc.).	**2** Forget to add contact information.
3 Offer different language versions to appeal to international visitors.	**3** Make a corporate website too heavy to load.

Expert information by
Martin Cedergren, Forsman & Bodenfors

Volvo – The Heart of Volvo

Agency
Forsman & Bodenfors

Designed by
Forsman & Bodenfors

Developed by
Forsman & Bodenfors

Production by
Kokokaka, itiden, Astronaut

Software
Adobe Creative Suite, After Effects, Flash, Soft Image

Awards
FWA Site Of The Day, New York Festivals, Epica

Launched
2006

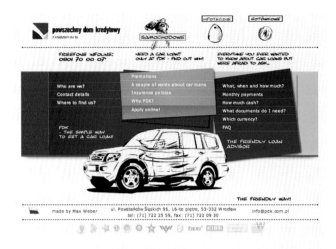

PDK

Agency
Max Weber

Designed by
Grzegorz Mogilewski,
Mateusz Subieta

Developed by
Lukasz Dyszy

Software
Flash

Awards
FWA Site Of The Month,
Cannes Cyber Lion
Gold, Silver Drum, New
York Festivals, Cresta,
KTR Award, Zloty Orzel,
Shortlisted at FWA/Adobe
Most Influential Flash Site
Of The Decade, Webby
Awards finalist, D&AD
Awards, LIAA, Epica

Launched
2004

www.pdk.pl/index_feng.html

The Vodafone Journey

Agency
North Kingdom

Designed by
Robert Lindström

Developed by
Klas Kroon

Software
Flash, Photoshop,
After Effects.

Awards
FWA Site Of The Day,
Finalist London International
Advertising Awards

Launched
2006

http://demo.northkingdom.
com/vodafonejourney

With the rise of eBay and PayPal stores, many people now have a PayPal account and are already comfortable using it to purchase online. Along with providing great security, one of the key benefits of having this option is that the account can be available to people that may not be eligible for a credit card (people under 18 years of age, for example).

Credit card vendors like 2Checkout make it very simple to add professional features to an e-commerce site, with the ability to add strong security for your customers and to get fraud reports on every purchase made, protecting you from users with stolen credit cards.

Do	Don't
1 Ensure your customer's payment details are protected; this is the single, most important part of any e-commerce business.	1 Sit back and think, "That wouldn't happen to me." Online fraud is rife and you should research as much as possible about security before launching your site.
2 Protect yourself by monitoring your sales closely and try to pick out patterns from fraudsters.	2 Assume your user is experienced online.
3 Keep the payment form as simple as possible, offering hints and examples where needed.	3 Offer only one payment method. The more payment methods you have, the more people will be able to purchase from you.

Expert information by
Jay Birch, AdvanceFlash

Teddies in Space

Agency
247 MediaStudios

Designed/Developed by
Ingo J. Ramin

Software
Photoshop, After Effects,
Flash, Cinema 4D

Awards
FWA Site Of The Day,
London International
Awards 2006

Launched
2006

www.teddiesinspace.com

The first thing you need when creating a product site is to figure out what your client is planning and why he is doing a site at all (and to help him/her understand it).

Then imagine yourself as a "target" surfer and find an innovative, explosive approach to show your client's product from an absolute new point of view. Be on the sharp edge.

Only after the "thinking" step has been fulfilled, begin to create, plan your interaction, construct the technical base for the project and get a team of professionals to implement your original concept.

Do

1
Think globally.
Always keep in mind
the final cut.

2
Look into yesterday
and step into
tomorrow. Don't be
afraid of choosing
experimental ways of
solving your problem.

3
Be a teamplayer.
A well-coordinated
team of talented
professionals is
the best way to
guarantee success.

Don't

1
Forget about your
client and your
mission. Whatever
you do — don't forget
you're creating a
product site, not just
something for your
own fun.

2
Neglect the time of
your busy site visitor,
as well as limitations
of his/her hardware
(and software).

3
Die by the keyboard.
There's no honour
in working 72 hours
without rest.

Expert information by
Vasily Lebedev, Red Keds Creative Agency

Product Display

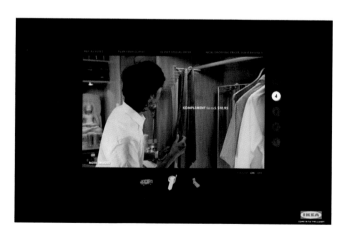

IKEA – Come into the closet

Agency
Forsman & Bodenfors

Designed by
Forsman & Bodenfors

Developed by
Forsman & Bodenfors,
Kokokaka, Camp David

Software
Adobe CS, After Effects,
Flash, Maya

Awards
FWA Site Of The Day,
Eurobest

Launched
2006

http://demo.fb.se/e/ikea/
comeintothecloset/site/
default.htm

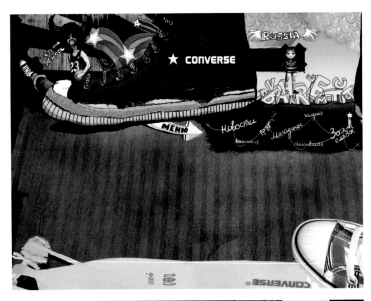

Converse Russia

Agency
Red Keds Creative Agency

Designed by
Stepan "Freeger" Bourlakov

Developed by
Vasily "Bazil" Lebedev

Software
Flash, Photoshop, Illustrator,
Corel Painter, 3ds Max,
Scite|Flash, Komodo, Moho,
After Effects, Particle Illusion

Awards
FWA Site Of The Day,
Styleboost

Launched
2007

www.converserussia.ru

UNIQLO

Agency
tha ltd.

Designed/Developed by
Yugo Nakamura

Software
Flash

Awards
FWA Site Of The Day

Launched
2006

www.uniqlo.com/us

Promotional Sites spread the word about a product or service. Some are short lived microsites that run for the duration of a campaign or a seasonal promotion. Some are larger websites that evolve over the course of time, with fresh content updated on a regular or semi-regular basis.

The web can be a cost effective alternative to traditional promotional efforts such as television, print and outdoor advertising. Promotional websites are growing more popular as marketers seek less expensive ways to reach larger audiences.

Effective promotional sites concisely communicate information in clever ways with the use of intuitive interactivity, full-motion video, animation, sound design, compelling graphics and quite often contests, games and sweepstakes.

Do

1
Attempt to captivate your audience within the first 2–5 seconds.

2
Communicate your most important message clearly and right up front.

3
Think about what your audience hopes to gain from visiting your site.

Don't

1
Weigh down the experience with heavy files and long load times.

2
Forget to include easy-to-find contact information.

3
Sacrifice substance for style.

Expert information by
Mark Ferdman, Freedom Interactive Design

Would You Like A Website?

Agency
Freedom Interactive Design

Designed/Developed by
Freedom Interactive

Software
Flash, After Effects

Awards
FWA Site Of The Day

Launched
2006

www.wouldyoulikeawebsite.com

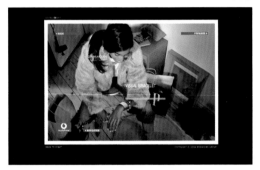

Vodafone Future Vision

Agency
North Kingdom

Designed by
Robert Lindström

Developed by
Martin Klasson

Software
Flash, Photoshop

Awards
FWA Site Of The Year, FWA
People's Choice Award,
Cannes Cyber Lions Gold
x2, One Show Interactive
Gold x2, New York Festivals
Gold x2, Corporate
Information, LIA Gold

Launched
2004

http://demo.northkingdom.
com/vodafonefuturevision

Kalles – Design Tube

Agency
Forsman & Bodenfors

Designed by
Forsman & Bodenfors

Developed by
Forsman & Bodenfors

Production by
B-Reel

Software
Adobe CS, After Effects,
Flash, Maya

Awards
FWA Site Of The Day, D&AD

Launched
2006

When selling a service it's all about the pros and cons, the good and the bad — pick your strategy and stay focused.

Media rich environments, forums and interactive websites allow consumers to explore possibilities, get questions answered, be sold benefits and services and most importantly — feel involved.

We can use real stories to sell real services, offer practical advice and solutions to problems. You have a captive audience and they're not restricted by time like a TV spot, so let them have fun exploring.

So whether you're publicly informing, gently persuading or hitting hard to convince — you can't always avoid those burning issues that consumers want answered — "Will it do this?" or "Why can't I do that!"

Do

1
Listen to consumers — market research can be a useful and powerful tool.

2
Try to think openly — don't worry about the technology, you'll always find someone clever enough to help you get the solution you want.

3
Come up with ways to capture your audience and keep them interested enough to explore your project and all the hard work that's been put in.

Don't

1
Get tied up with one or two elements; try to give equal effort to the whole project.

2
Try to answer every question you and your client can think of — concentrate on getting a few clear messages right.

3
Be afraid of having fun and mixing media — video, Flash, and Photoshop make a great team.

Expert information by
Owen Johnson, Moseleywebb

Atlantis

Agency
Firstborn

Designed/Developed by
Firstborn

Software
Flash, Flash Video, XML
database generated from
CMS, .NET C#, MS SQL
Server 2000 Database,
Akamai Optimization

Awards
FWA Site Of The Day

Launched
2005

www.fborn.com/
websites/140_atlantis/
flash.htm

E-Commerce

The Broadband Journal

Agency
Moseleywebb

Designed by
Owen Johnson

Developed by
Innivo

Software
Photoshop, Illustrator,
After Effects, Flash,
Dreamweaver, PHP, MySQL

Awards
FWA Site Of The Day,
Adobe Site Of The Day

Philips Home Entertainment

Agency
North Kingdom

Designed by
Robert Lindström

Developed by
Stefan Thomson

Software
Flash, Photoshop, 3ds Max

Awards
FWA Site Of The Month,
EPICA Bronze

Launched
2004

http://demo.northkingdom.
com/philips

Secured transferring of sensitive data, such as credit card numbers and personal information, is imperative for all e-commerce sites. SSL (Secured Sockets Layer) is a protocol that allows data to be encrypted for safe transmittal. Although potentially the least visible to the end user, it is by far the most important piece for online shopping.

Do

1
Make sure the Registrant information (mailing address) of the domain matches your Organizational information (DUNS number or other official document such as a Sales Tax License) before ordering your certificate.

2
Use at least 128 bit encryption. Protecting consumer's privacy and online shopping safety is vital.

3
Initiate your SSL session immediately for Flash sites.

Don't

1
Wait too long. Changes to DNS information and ordering SSL certificates can take up to 92 hours.

2
Sacrifice security for budget. Go with a reliable vendor that can assure both quality certificates and maximum compatibility.

3
Reuse certificates. Each secured domain should have its own unique certificate for valid authentication.

Expert information by
Ian Coyle, FL2

E-Commerce
SSL

Kobalt Shop

Agency
Kobalt60

Designed by
Bang, Dongwook

Developed by
Lee, Sangmook

Software
Flash, Photoshop

Awards
FWA Site Of The Day,
Korea Web Awards

Launched
2005

www.kobaltshop.com

PROTECT YOUR DATA | MIMOBOTS
The limited edition Star Wars mimots are here. Choose Darth Vader, a Stormtrooper, R2-D2 or Chewbacca to store and transfer your files, music or pictures. Comes loaded with plenty of attitude and exclusive Star Wars content.

VIEW FULL PRODUCT LINE

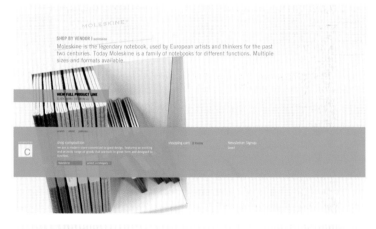

SHOP BY VENDOR | moleskine
Moleskine is the legendary notebook, used by European artists and thinkers for the past two centuries. Today Moleskine is a family of notebooks for different functions. Multiple sizes and formats available.

VIEW FULL PRODUCT LINE

SHOPPING CART | review your cart

Shop Composition

Agency
Hello-Sexy, FL2

Designed/Developed by
Ian Coyle

Software
Flash, Photoshop, asp.net

Awards
FWA Site Of The Day, Clio Shortlist, Communication Arts Interactive Annual, Flash Forward Finalist, SXSW Interactive Finalist, Forbes Best of Web

Launched
2005

Shop Spicebox:
Spice Up Someone's Life

Agency
Kindness and Humility

Designed/Developed by
Chris Erickson

Software
Flash

Awards
FWA Site Of The Day

Launched
2006

Afterword

by Lars Bastholm, AKQA

word

After

From Theory to Practice

Congratulations! If you made it all the way to this afterword, it means that you're passionate about wanting to create great digital experiences, whether it's for yourself or for a client. That's a great start, because without that passion, it's not going to happen.

You've just heard from a group of people who really know what they are talking about. They fought the wars in the trenches – they've seen their ideas crippled by colleagues and clients who didn't know any better, yet they crawled back, bleeding, when they didn't succeed – then they came back for more, like punch-drunk fighters who didn't know how to say stop.

The websites you've seen in this book were not easy to create. They took blood, sweat and tears to get to the point where both the client and the creative team were happy to say, "It's done." It took a vision that survived the journey from doodles on a piece of paper and through countless "what ifs" to an almost miraculous finish: a website that was deemed good enough to be included in this book. Allow me to congratulate each and every one whose work is in this book. I know how rarely the stars align to make a fantastic idea become a reality.

> "It's hard work to create a good website, let alone a successful one. So when you succeed in making it, remember to celebrate properly and enjoy it."

OK, so you've made the decision that you want to create digital experiences. Where do you start? Let's say that you sat down and taught yourself Photoshop, Flash, and a few other programs, just to get the basic skills nailed. And you've read this book. Now, you are staring at a white piece of paper, your eyes are so dry that it feels like they could start bleeding any second. Still, nothing comes to mind, and you keep staring…

So where do ideas come from? If you ever want to make a creative person shut up and glare threateningly at you, that's the question to ask. Not because they don't want to tell you, but because most of the time, they have no idea. That's why coming up with ideas is the hardest thing to teach anybody, as ideas are usually a by-product of the sum total of your experiences in life. So let's not jump into that particular black box, but let's talk about how to find inspiration instead. Of course, you can go to websites like The FWA and see what other people are doing and stand in awe of their skills and vision, but often truly original thoughts will come from going completely outside of your field, say, by picking up a copy of "New Advances in Orthodontics" or "Trucker Monthly" at your local magazine shop or by going to a NASCAR race. In fact, anything that gets you away from the computer. Yes, I'm sorry, but you do sometimes have to leave the computer.

"Often truly original thoughts will come from going completely outside of your field, say, by picking up a copy of 'New Advances in Orthodontics' or 'Trucker Monthly' at your local magazine shop or by going to a NASCAR race."

Other times, your idea comes through a series of coincidences. A few years ago, I was sitting in a pub in London with my creative partner, staring out of the window while sipping a pint. We had just finished a photo shoot for Nike that same day. Nike was getting ready to launch *Nike Shox*, a technology that they had spent over 15 years developing, and was naturally anxious to launch in the best possible manner. We had done the bits for the basketball version of the shoe, and that same day we'd finished the cross-training shoot. All good, except there were only three weeks left until we had to launch the website to coincide with a major global campaign. And we still didn't know how to bring the third shoe in the series, the running shoe, to life on the web. We ordered another round. The news was on the TV in the corner of the bar, and they were interviewing two joggers in Hyde Park. The two runners that they were interviewing were so winded by their run that they could barely speak, and they sounded very funny. We began riffing on tricky situations to get interviewed in, where even the smartest person would have a hard time making sense: on the can, while having sex, while running the marathon. Wait…

Cut to two weeks later. I'm sitting in a hotel in New York with a tape recorder hooked up to a phone. Every 20 minutes, I'm calling five people, all of whom are running the New York Marathon in Nike Shox shoes. They are equipped with self-answering mobile phones and a cord from the phone taped to their body and plugged into their ear. This allows me to interview them about how they are doing in the race while they are running, without them having to change their pace or do anything differently than they normally would. My favourite exchange was this one. **Question:** "So, how are you doing?" **Answer:** "I just got overtaken by a guy wearing a chicken suit, so probably not so good." At the same time, we had photographers along the route taking pictures of our runners. They all made it across the finishing line. One with a new personal best, some not so good. The whole thing was then edited together into an interactive experience where you could check in with the five different runners at different stages of the run and hear how they were doing. It was probably the closest you'll ever get to experience a marathon run without actually having to run it. It was the culmination of two weeks of insane work to make this crazy idea happen, finding the runners, persuading them to break in a new pair of shoes in record time, making sure the technology would work etc. The fact that it happened at all was something of a miracle. It's one of the projects I'm the most proud of having been involved in. It also won a couple of awards, so I guess other people liked it too.

My final piece of advice is that you want to make a lot of talented friends. These days, building a digital experience is very much like creating a movie. You have a group of people with various skills that need to work very closely together. It's rarely a one-man job – well, not unless you happen to be annoyingly talented like Dave Werner *(see chapter 2, category: Portfolios – Personal)*, whose student portfolio set the agency world on fire in a veritable hiring frenzy, as Dave appeared to have been born fully formed and ready to go to work. But that's the exception. We mere mortals have to corral the troops and make sure the original vision survives through the various stages of a project until it gets released on the unsuspecting public. Hopefully to great acclaim.

> **"These days, building a digital experience is very much like creating a movie. You have a group of people with various skills that need to work very closely together."**

It's hard work to create a good website, let alone a successful one. So when you succeed in making it, remember to celebrate properly and enjoy it. The next one doesn't get any easier. But if you are passionate about it, like me and the other people you've met in this book, you probably can't imagine doing anything else.

Have fun and good luck.

Lars Bastholm
AKQA

Bio.
Lars Bastholm
AKQA

When AKQA opened its doors in New York in 2004, Lars Bastholm was placed at the helm as Executive Creative Director. Lars has been working in the interactive marketing industry for over 12 years. After starting up Grey Interactive in Scandinavia, he joined Framfab in Copenhagen, Denmark as creative director. There he worked on some of the world's most recognised brands, including Nike, LEGO, Sprite, and Carlsberg. At AKQA New York, Lars currently works on such brands as Coca-Cola, Smirnoff, and Comcast.

He is one of the most award-winning creatives in digital marketing with a large number of respected international awards to his name, including 3 Cannes Cyber Lions Grand Prix.

Lars has served as juror on most major award shows and is a member of The International Academy of Digital Arts and Sciences. Lars was recently featured in the book *How to Catch the Big Idea: The Strategy of Top Creatives*.
–
www.akqa.com

"My final piece of advice is that you want to make a lot of talented friends."

mono
USA
mono-1.com
monoface
(Make People Smile)
99

Moraes, Pedro
Brazil
pedromoraes.net
Adhemas.com
(Graphic Quality)
183

Mortierbrigade
Belgium
mortierbrigade.com
Sprite Test Laboratories
(Entertain)
85
Mortierbrigade
(Aliased Text)
175

Moseleywebb
Wales, UK
moseleywebb.com
The Broadband Journal
(Selling a Service)
284

MSLK
USA
mslk.com
M Studio
(Navigation – Hidden
Menus)
43

Nn.

Natzke Design
USA
natzkedesign.com
Comcastic
(Fullscreen)
25

Neave, Paul
England
neave.com
(Dynamic)
142
Flash Earth
(Dynamic)
145
Neave.tv
(Streaming & Progressive
Loading)
204

Neostream Interactive
Australia/South Korea
neostream.com
Neostream Interactive
(Have Attitude)
93

Neue Digitale
Germany
neue-digitale.de
adidas Sport Style Y-3
Cubes
(Navigation – Animated
Menus)
39
adidas Originals
(Showreels & Motion
Graphics)
241

Noble, Rob
Lightmaker Group
England/USA
lightmaker.com
(Usability)
206

Noe, Dan
USA
noedesign.com
Noe Design
(Portfolios – Personal)
114

North Kingdom
Sweden
northkingdom.com
Cork Up Your Sandwich
(Colour)
23
Toyota – AYGO
(Create Surprise)
79
North Kingdom
(Portfolios – Agency)
109
Planet In Need
(Broadband)
137
The Vodafone Journey
(Corporate)
271
Vodafone Future Vision
(Promotional Sites)
280
Philips Home Entertainment
(Selling a Service)
285

number 9
USA
number9.com
Comcastic
(Fullscreen)
25

Nutility
South Korea
nutility.co.kr
The New Carnival
(3D)
21

Oo.

Oshyn Inc.
USA
oshyn.com
Volkswagen
of America
(Search Inside the Page)
155

Pp.

Palmer, Rick
BLOC
England
blocmedia.com
(Newsletter)
100

Paschke, Susanne
Germany
susannepaschke.de
Susanne Paschke
(Art & Illustration)
224

Perfect Fools
Sweden
perfectfools.com
Saab Pilots Wanted
(Entertain)
84

pill & pillow
Hong Kong
pillandpillow.com
Forgotten War
(Photography Archive)
194

Pop
USA
pop.us
New Super Mario Bros
(Typeface)
60

Preloaded
England
preloaded.com
Tongsville
(Navigation – Horizontal)
47
Death in Sakkara
(Games)
179

Prieto, Juan Carlos
Enigmind Ltda
Colombia
enigmind.com
(Language Choice)
188

Purgason, Todd
JUXT Interactive
USA
juxtinteractive.com
(Community)
226

Rr.

Red Interactive Agency
USA
ff0000.com
Junior's Giants
(Intros)
29
UFC 66
(Sport)
248

Red Keds Creative Agency
Russia
redkeds.com
Converse Russia
(Product Display)
276

Richter7
USA
richter7.com
Hope Garden
(Good Causes)
89

Robinizer
Germany
robinizer.de
Steffen Jahn
(Minimalist)
36

Rozbicki, Bartłomiej
Ars Thanea
Poland
arsthanea.com
(Aliased Text)
172

RTT AG
Germany/USA
rtt.ag
(Video Quality)
208
Audi R8
(Video Quality)
210

First of all, I must say a huge thank you to Benedikt Taschen for his amazing publishing company, TASCHEN, which has vision and passion – and for saying "yes" to this book; Julius Wiedemann, whom I have grown to know as a friend – without his patience and guidance this book would never have happened; KentLyons and Jon Cefai for the wonderful book design, and Daniel Siciliano Brêtas for his excellent attention to detail. Not forgetting the numerous other members of TASCHEN with whom I have corresponded whilst finalising the other aspects of this book. Last but not least, I must take a moment to thank Jürgen Dubau for proofreading the German language version; Benjamin Laugel and Olivier Marchand for the French version and Hugo Olivera for the Spanish version.

Rob Ford

Firstly, a big thanks to Rob, who worked tirelessly, giving us the best content and advice for completing this book. Huge thanks go to Daniel Siciliano Brêtas, for his great coordination and attention to detail; the guys at KentLyons, especially Jon Cefai for his commitment and great design – always understanding the vision for the book. You guys do an amazing job. Thanks also to Chris Mizsak, for his insights on improving the text. Lastly, to all the contributors without whom this book wouldn't have been possible. You all do such amazing work and we want to make sure that it inspires people all over the world.

Julius Wiedemann

© 2011 TASCHEN GmbH
Hohenzollernring 53
D-50672 Köln
www.taschen.com

Original edition:
© 2008 TASCHEN GmbH

Editor
Rob Ford
Julius Wiedemann
Editorial Coordination
Daniel Siciliano Brêtas

Design by KentLyons
Cover design by Sense/Net Art Direction, Andy Disl and Birgit Eichwede, Cologne, www.sense-net.net

Production
Stefan Klatte

Printed in South Korea
ISBN 978-3-8365-2812-2

TASCHEN is not responsible when web address cannot be reached if they are offline or can be viewed just with plug-ins.